'The strength of this book is tl (often confusing) "practical" an congregations when their pastoi head on – the complex "emotio.... uynamics of such a transition for those left behind. Managing these well is the key to making confident and creative appointments.'

Father Alan Gyle, Diocese of London

'In writing *How to Make Great Appointments in the Church* Claire and Su have done a great service to the Church. If you are involved in a church appointment process in any way, this book will guide you from beginning to end. The style is clear and easy to read and here you will discover methods to select a person who is called, competent and likely to have the right chemistry to fit into your team. It's just like having your own personal coach and mentor to guide you through what can be difficult terrain. Above all Claire and Su will help you focus the process on God and help you to turn selection and interviewing into a real process of vocational discernment.

'If you are a potential leader, thinking about a move, read here for insight on thinking and praying through the process. It will lead you to the right questions to ask, and show you how to go about discerning your own gifts and skills as well as preparing for interview. And, again, it will help you focus on where God might be leading you.'

The Revd Stephen Adams,
Dean of Ministry Development,
St Michael's College, Llandaff, Cardiff

'The regularity with which churches replace their pastoral staff poses a dilemma: it is regular enough to warrant this sort of guide, but infrequent enough to ensure that the group responsible last time a vacancy occurred has changed so much that a guide of this sort is required reading. For this reason alone, such a book deserves wide usage. However, to its utility is added the sheer wisdom of its approach, and I think this resource will prove an invaluable guide for churches of many differing traditions. Even if the default language is Anglican, the processes it describes will prove readily transferable to others, such as Baptists or Congregationalists. I recommend it to all church congregations facing the prospect of calling a new minister.'

The Revd Dr Paul Goodliff, Head of Ministry for the Baptist Union of Great Britain and Moderator of its National Settlement Team

'Discerning the best way through a change of ministerial appointment is challenging and complex for churches and ministers alike. This book gives clear, practical guidelines that will help both parties to avoid common pitfalls and achieve an outcome that is both right and fair. Churches and clergy in all denominations will find valuable pointers and timely warnings.'

The Revd Dr Richard Clutterbuck, Principal, Edgehill Theological College, Belfast

'This excellent book will help your church make the right choices about church staff. Packed with wisdom, experience and humility. Make sure your church has a copy.'

Dr Krish Kandiah, Executive Director: Churches in Mission, at the Evangelical Alliance

'*How to Make Great Appointments in the Church* is a valuable new resource for parishes looking to appoint a new minister. It offers some very thoughtful and creative advice on some of the processes that can seem daunting, like undertaking an audit of where the church is and where it might need to go under God, as a way of preparing to write an honest and helpful parish profile.

'It is good to see frequent mention of the importance of prayer; of the collaborative nature of the task; of the pitfalls to avoid in writing a person profile; and of the need to look forward hopefully and confidently to the new things God might have in store.

'Read alongside any specific guidance offered by your particular denomination, *How to Make Great Appointments in the Church* is a very practical and useful guide to this most important process. It will be useful to church members, to candidates seeking new posts, and to those who work with the local on behalf of the wider church.'

The Rt Revd Alan Winton, Bishop of Thetford

'Having been involved in appointments within the Christian Church, secular institutions and voluntary organizations this book is superb in the guidelines it offers, with wisdom, integrity, discernment and practical application. While written with appointments of clergy and ministers in mind the contents can be applied to other disciplines. It considers the needs in depth of all parties preparing for, interviewing and welcoming the new appointee. It is worth buying in quantity and following step by step as its development scratches everyone where they are itching at each stage of the process, thus calming their nerves and allaying their fears.'

The Very Revd John Richardson, Diocese of Rochester

'Invaluable, practical wisdom to help us in what is the most vital decision for a local church: the selection and appointment of new leadership. With step-by-step strategies, encouragements to prayerful reflection and creative use of story, the authors take us by the hand and help us through what can be a minefield. This is a book that is needed in every church, everywhere, whatever the denomination or brand. Highly recommended.'

Jeff Lucas, author, speaker, broadcaster

'Claire and Su have come up with a valuable resource for the life of the Church. In their writing and thinking this work is incisive, practical, very readable and easy to follow. And it's thought provoking. I found the way they unpacked "Calling, Competence and Chemistry" cut across boundaries and opened up a lot of creative thinking. Whatever your theological outlook or your church tradition, you will find something in here that will be helpful. Key is its focus on the importance of prayerfulness. It's also got some good stuff in it on dealing with difficult issues. My church is currently in a vacancy and looking for a new minister. This book has helped me clarify our thinking about how we move forward together.'

Geoff Hammond, Reader, Diocese of Chelmsford

'The discernment of the right leader, God's person, for a congregation and community is pivotal to creative ministry in the service of God's mission. Claire and Su write from their own professional and Christian experience about the issues and the process. Their insights will help all those involved in any way. They explain not only what should happen, but also why, and remind us of the contribution every person makes in what must be a partnership in prayer, service and discerning.'

The Rt Revd Christopher Foster, Bishop of Portsmouth

Claire Pedrick is a coach who began her career working for an ecumenical organization. She has been a selector for the Methodist World Church Office and CMS, and has trained people in vocational selection for the past 25 years. Su Blanch is an HR consultant with 15 years' experience in corporate life.

Claire and Su both work for 3D Coaching. Part of their work involves coaching clergy at all levels to fill out good applications and be their best at interview. They have both spoken on vocation at Spring Harvest, attend local Anglican churches and recently have been involved in appointing new vicars.

SPCK Library of Ministry

HOW TO MAKE GREAT APPOINTMENTS IN THE CHURCH

Calling, Competence and Chemistry

SPCK Library of Ministry

CLAIRE PEDRICK and SU BLANCH

First published in Great Britain in 2011

Society for Promoting Christian Knowledge
36 Causton Street
London SW1P 4ST
www.spckpublishing.co.uk

The author and publisher have made every effort to ensure that the
external website and email addresses included in this book are correct and up
to date at the time of going to press. The author and publisher are not responsible
for the content, quality or continuing accessibility of the sites.

British Library Cataloguing-in-Publication Data
A catalogue record for this book is available from the British Library

ISBN 978–0–281–06419–9

1 3 5 7 9 10 8 6 4 2

Typeset by Graphicraft Ltd, Hong Kong
Printed in Great Britain by MPG Books Group

Produced on paper from sustainable forests

To Father Alan Gyle of the Diocese of London, who encouraged us to write this book, and to Revds Simon and Louise Moore of St Paul's Church, Letchworth, and Revd Dr David Munchin of St Mary's Church, Welwyn, whose appointments to our own churches gave us a story to tell

Contents

Illustrations

Figures

Tables

Foreword

Church appointments are always fraught with an infuriating mix of dullness and danger and this guide is long, long overdue. We have moved from an eighteenth-century world where the right claret and the hand of the bishop's daughter were a guide to ecclesiastical preferment to a different territory where secular practice meets amateur wisdom and God's hand can seem just as absent. No matter what the Christian denomination, there is something here for everyone to learn and lean on with sensible advice and a good smattering of anecdote and humour. The Church, along with large elements in society, is replacing old-style 'trust' with 'transparency', and authority with democracy, presuming that it will deliver a fairer outcome. This is not necessarily true because all parties can become actors in the theatre of appointments, as is so clearly brought out by the authors. However, prayer is at the centre of this excellent guide, and when we expose ourselves honestly to this refining fire the first question we are asked is about ourselves and our personal prejudices. As Pedrick and Blanch say, 'We are the body of Christ . . . And like Jesus' first team, we are not all good at everything!'

John Lee, Clergy Appointments Adviser, Church of England

Acknowledgements

Thanks

to the hundreds of ministers who have shared their stories of vocational discernment with us – on courses, in one-to-ones and in passing;

to the rest of the 3D team who have carried on the work while we have had our heads down;

to everyone who gave us technical feedback;

to SPCK for agreeing to the use of 'they' and 'their' rather than 'he or she' and 'his or her'.

Part 1
CONTEXT

1

Introduction

'The problem is,' said the man sitting next to us at breakfast, 'that we are a local ecumenical partnership looking for a new minister and we don't know whose process to use.'

Whether your church uses a formal process or no process to find a new minister, this book is for you. You will find a rigorous process which will help you appoint a new leader to your church who is called and competent and has good enough chemistry with your team to be able to lead you in your next season. Whether you call them a minister, vicar, presbyter, church leader or priest, if it's time for a new one there will be lots of voices telling you what to do and few helping you discern what kind of process will help your church make the most fitting appointment.

Here's a possible scenario. It came as a shock when your loved and respected leader spoke with you and confirmed that they were leaving to become the minister of a lovely church by the sea. This person had been in post for many years, and the congregation had rather expected that they would continue in post for many more years. Everyone seemed so comfortable. The boat was not expecting to be rocked.

So this may not be what you were anticipating. And if you have a leadership responsibility in the church as a deacon, elder, church steward or churchwarden, you are now in a position where you will be required to make some critical and possibly scary decisions on behalf of the church community. You feel a weight of expectation upon your shoulders. There could be processes that you have never heard of that now need to be put in place. The congregation suddenly feels frail and rudderless.

Alternatively, your minister is leaving and you are breathing a sigh of relief. Your church is now in a position to move on in a new and different way . . . But which way? Different groups in the congregation have varied ideas and positions. These diverse opinions may have been developing for many years and have been suppressed. There could be strong voices raised in the next few months. Some people in your church will already have a name in mind! Others will be looking for the opposite or the clone of your last leader. Yet others will be so upset that the last minister has left that they will be unable to think about who might come next.

Whatever the scenario you face as you move through this process, it will have its own specific fears and challenges. This may be the first time you have been involved in a process like this. And if not, the panorama now is probably very different from last time. You are certain that you want to do a good job, but how? You may have been sent some useful information from the diocese or region and have picked up information from others. What are the priorities and what do you need to think about first? How do you discern and select simultaneously?

The technical job of appointing a new leader to a church is only one step in a bigger process. Simon Barrington-Ward, a former bishop of Coventry, described clergy in a church as a team through time. Each needs skills to complement those who have gone before. The transition from one minister to the next, with the likelihood of a gap or vacancy or interregnum, is not a problem which needs to be solved but an opportunity for the church to begin considering bigger questions about where you are now.

Therefore, in this book we will explore:

- Who are you?
- Where are you now as a church?
- Where is your community now?
- Where might you be going?

Once you have reflected on these questions, the question changes to:

- Given who you are now, what kind of a leader do you need for the next season in your life?

And finally:

- Given who you need, what process will you use to find that person?

Good appointments depend on you discerning this first, communicating clearly who you are as a parish and then developing a good process involving both discernment and selection to clarify what kind of a minister you are looking for now.

In *The 7 Habits of Highly Effective People*, Stephen Covey recommends we 'begin with the end in mind'.[1] The end point is that, having made an appointment which has considered the calling, competence and chemistry of candidates, you have a new minister in your church who will be the person your church needs now and for the future.

As a church you may want to meet several candidates who all bring different gifts and skills to begin to discern who is the right person to lead you in the next part of your journey. Alternatively, you may be looking at people one at a time and your discernment is about whether this candidate is the right person for you. Either way, you are trying to discern who God is calling to be your next minister and the candidates are trying to discern whether your church is the right place for them. So it is a discernment and selection process for you all. Mindful of Covey, if the candidate is going to be offered a job by the end of the process or asked: 'If we were to offer the role to you, would you accept?', you will want them to discern well. That means that they, like you, will need to have space and time to process and think.

There are many who would be great leaders for your church and each might take you in a slightly different direction. But any minister will not do. This is not simply about churchmanship. Of course, a priest who values the sacraments and sees the retelling of the Christian story through High Mass as pivotal may not be the right leader of a church where there are no vestments and Communion is only celebrated once a month. Equally, not every leader who shares your churchmanship will be the right leader for the season that your church and community are now entering. Each step of the process must enable you to be clear on those who you are willing to take further into the discernment and selection process, and those whose skills and experience are not what your church needs for its next leader.

2

How to use this book

How it works

We think that there are three elements that are required for you to appoint the right minister: Calling, Competence and Chemistry. We are interested in how these specifically relate to your context. Is the candidate called to your church? Will they be competent enough to do the things you need? Is there a good enough chemistry between the candidate and the team?

We want to help you find candidates who will sit right in the centre of the diagram in Figure 2.1: those that have the calling, competence and chemistry to fit in your church context. A minister may feel called to your church and may have the skills you require, but may lack the qualities needed to work well with the team or the congregation. Or they may have the right skills (competence) and connection with the people (chemistry) but their vocation is not in your church setting. Alternatively, calling and chemistry may be just right, but they do not have the skills required to be able to do the jobs you need them to do.

The candidates you see will have demonstrated their calling and competence within the selection and training process for ministry.

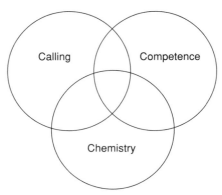

Figure 2.1 The elements of calling, competence and chemistry

Figure 2.2 The selection process

You can assume that they are called to ministry and competent enough to fulfil the general requirements of the role of minister. That does not mean that they will be right for your church in your context at this time.

In order for you to find out if they are the right person for you, you need to understand your setting. Figure 2.2 shows, very simply, the process which we will take you through in the book.

This process works on the assumption that unless you know enough about your church in its community you will not know who the right minister is, and therefore, even if that candidate does apply, you may not recognize that they are who you need.

What is the value of answering the 'Where are we now?' question? You know some things about your church and other people hold different knowledge. You may understand the buildings and the fabric of the church in great detail, but deeper and more fundamental questions about how the church operates and what its purpose is now need to be asked. Considering both the history and possible futures of the church will enable a much better understanding of who it is that needs to come in now and be the minister for the current and the future season.

Once you have that information, discerning who can take on this role is much simpler. There is a clear understanding of the context into which you are selecting. And once you understand who you need, you can then determine a process by which you can find and appoint that specific person.

This book will enable you to work through this process in a logical fashion (Fig. 2.3 overleaf). Each section has three parts to it, becoming more practical as you read through:

- Why is this important?
- Preparation.
- Action.

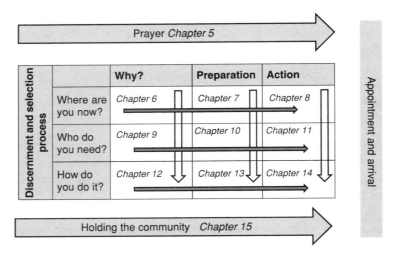

Figure 2.3 The structure of this book

We've written this book so that you can read it from start to finish. It may be that there are particular parts which you want to focus on. You could decide to understand all the theory in the 'why' chapters first, before moving on to preparation and action. For those readers who like to get on with the doing, we do suggest some time at least is spent on 'why' and preparation, if only to get a better perspective.

Who is the book for?

We've noticed that guides to appointments are often written in churchy language, yet the people who need to manage the process in the local context may not be fluent or comfortable in that. We hope that this book is practical, accessible and easy to use for all who might want to read it. Who might that be?

- *Church representatives*: those responsible for running the process and making local decisions about the next minister as well as bridging the gap. You will gain an overview of the process as well as finer details, thereby minimizing the risk of making a mistake. We are addressing church representatives as 'you'.
- *Regional representatives*: district chair, rural dean, archdeacon, team leader or bishop – you will want churches to have a good process yet may not have time to commit to helping them through every

step. You want to appoint ministers who are called and competent and where the chemistry between them and others will work well. This book will give you insight into what is happening at a detailed and local level and how this dovetails into your process.

- *Clergy candidates*: by understanding how discernment and selection works from the church's side, you can prepare in an informed way. As you read, consider how this will affect the way you complete application forms and plan for interviews or meetings. There are also sections which are specifically written for you so that you can be ready to give the local church what they need to make a decision based on discernment and selection.
- *Clergy in post*: in order to run a robust discernment and selection process, the first step is to find out 'Where are we now?' This question can be usefully asked at other times, particularly if you see a season of change and uncertainty ahead. By following the 'Where are we now?' stream, you will be able to facilitate an audit of your church which could be used for many purposes. This is also useful preparation for writing role descriptions.
- *Ministers recruiting team members in their church*: the principles used in this book apply to other appointments including youth workers and pastoral assistants, for example.
- *Those involved in discerning vocations and selection to ordained ministry*: the interviewing chapters will be helpful for people in this role.

Different denominations have different processes and they all involve exploring calling, competence and chemistry in some way. Not all of this material will be needed for every church's process. Some churches will not use competitive interviews and some will not use auditions. For those churches who see candidates one at a time, not all the information we provide about the selection event will be relevant. However, understanding the purpose of all the steps will widen your perspective and give insights into how your process will work and what needs to be included. We suggest that reading 'Why?' will be helpful as you prepare your discernment process.

3

Discernment and selection

Discernment is difficult enough for people trying to find their own vocational journey. It is even more of a challenge to try and discern someone else's. When we talk about vocation to work, Aristotle's wisdom, 'Where your talents and the needs of the world collide, there lies your vocation', can be useful. Talents are a combination of strengths and passions.

So if the strengths and passions of the candidate overlap with the needs of your church and community now (Fig. 3.1), then this might indicate their calling to your context. Testing a call is an inexact science. Selection has tick lists and objective measurements. Discernment requires faithfulness and listening, and is shared by the candidate, stakeholders (that is, those impacted by the decision) and your church and community. This process continues the discernment and selection process for ministry in the Church. This time it is about calling to a specific context at this stage of the candidate's ministry.

Discernment may not give you black-and-white answers. It is always worthwhile to ask a question, but not always necessary to answer it.

You may come with extensive experience of interviewing from your day job. Vocational selection is different because you will need to hold

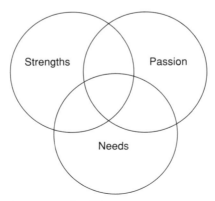

Figure 3.1 The elements of calling

pragmatic questions about competence and chemistry in creative tension with prayer, discernment and exploration of the Holy Spirit's calling. Vocational selection is like building a jigsaw. Your church and other stakeholders need enough of the picture to be reasonably confident that the candidate is both called and competent enough to be appointed to your post. That picture will be drawn from a combination of paperwork, prayer, references and encounters.

It can be a challenge to interviewers who have discerned through prayer who the right candidate might be and are then faced at interview with someone who doesn't match this. If you feel that God may be calling a particular individual, you still need to find pragmatic evidence to back that up. A prayerful process alone is a risk. How do you know you're right? How do you discern the voice of God through everyone's own preferences and prejudices? Equally, a non-prayerful process is a risk as it pays no attention to discernment. God needs to be present in the process and cannot be left outside the door while the real business is attended to. You may need to challenge yourselves from time to time – 'Where is God in this process?' or 'Where is the evidence in this process?' – to ensure that you are maintaining the balance appropriately.

When we talk to candidates, we help them learn how to give you evidence of their skills and vision, both on paper and when they meet you. The biggest challenge for clergy is to talk about their gifts and skills. They are often disfluent and uncomfortable in doing this at depth, yet this is what you need from them to make an informed decision.

There is always going to be a tension between a process that serves your needs and one that is as comfortable as possible for the candidates. To work effectively, the whole process needs to contain:

- a realistic audit of where you are now and what you need;
- a discernment process, under God, to find your next leader;
- a selection process for you to establish whether a potential candidate fits what you need sufficiently well to be your new minister.

Different processes

Both language and process in discernment and selection vary across denominations and even within individual churches. In general, the process is likely to include:

- a discernment process
- paperwork – theirs and yours
- a face-to-face encounter
- an audition.

These four steps are common to most churches (Table 3.1).

In most denominations there is a balance between sending and calling. In independent churches calling has the upper hand, whereas the Salvation Army (as we understand it) simply sends its officers without much input from the local corps. The Church of England and the Methodist Church in Britain are somewhere in between. One-at-a-time is often a sending system where the people making the decision have profiles to look at.

What is the local unit of church and mission? In the Church of England it is the diocese, and the local vicar shares their ministry with the bishop. In the British Methodist Church the circuit is the local unit and so the balance of the ministerial team in a particular circuit will be an important criterion when a new appointment is made. What happens liturgically when a new minister is inducted says a lot about this relationship with the wider Church.

Baptists, Methodists and some Anglican churches (commonly about 50 per cent of Crown appointments) meet candidates one at a time. There is selection in these encounters. After all, at the end of your encounter you will need to make a decision about whether to invite this person to be your new minister or whether to look at someone else.

Processes where a number of candidates are considered at the same time need to be carefully handled to ensure that they do not turn into competitive events. You do not want to be judging who is the best of the bunch: it may be that none of them are right for your church now and the process then needs to be reviewed and started again.

Occasionally a regional minister or bishop will ask someone to go to a particular church almost as an act of obedience, knowing that the person is a good fit for the role in this season. Equally, some ministers may be of the mindset: 'Put me where you want me to be.' For them, the new world of applications is a challenge and they do not willingly scour the clergy appointments adverts. And there are some places where independent churches can choose their own process.

Table 3.1 Selection across different churches

Denomination	Style	Discernment process	Paperwork	Interview	Audition	Stakeholders
Baptist	One-at-a-time	✓	Church profile/ministerial profile	One-at-a-time	Preaching with a view	Deacons, moderator, regional minister
Methodist	Matching and one-at-a-time	✓	Stationing profile: minister and circuit appointment	Meeting with church stewards		Church stewards, circuit stewards, circuit invitations committee, district lay stationing representatives, stationing matching group
Church of Scotland	Interview process and one-at-a-time	✓	Parish profile Application or recommendation	With nominating committee	Nominating committee listen to preaching Preferred candidate leads service for whole congregation	Presbytery, Ministries Council give permission to call Interim moderator, nominating committee (13)
Church of England	Interview process	✓	Parish profile Application form	With more than one candidate	Panel listen to preaching	Parish representative, patron, archdeacon, bishop
Church of England when patron is Crown, Lord Chancellor and some other independent patrons	One-at-a-time (about 50 per cent of roles) 50 per cent through standard diocesan system (see above)	✓	Meeting with Crown appointments secretary or patron	Meeting with Crown appointments secretary and other stakeholders – one at a time		Parish representative Patron Archdeacon, bishop
Independent	Various	✓	You decide	You decide	You decide	You decide
Our church						

A common language

Across the Church, people use different languages to describe processes, skills and tools, depending on where they sit in church tradition, theology or practice. It is impossible to find a common language, and even within one denomination there is such a variety of understandings that it is a struggle to find a vocabulary with which all are comfortable. And that is before you include denominations and independent churches.

Depending on the church, new ministers are 'given a charge', are 'called' or are 'stationed' or 'appointed'. If we were to use language which was relevant to every situation you would soon lose your way. For example, 'When you meet your new vicar/priest/presbyter/ leader/incumbent/minister/pastor, you will find that . . .' is rather awkward. Therefore, we will be using generic language, as in Table 3.2, and hope that you will read this book in a way which connects with your own context.

Table 3.2 How we use language in the book

Audition	Preaching with a view; presentation; homily
Candidate	The person looking at your role
Church council	Wider sub-group who may be trustees responsible for church. They may not all be in the interview room but will wish to be involved in some way; e.g. parochial church council (PCC)
Church representatives	Handful of individuals responsible for leading the appointment process, e.g. parish representatives, churchwardens, church stewards, elders, deacons, leadership team, nominating committee
Minister	Vicar, priest, incumbent, presbyter, pastor, minister, church leader, stipendiary minister, rector
Parish profile	The document which describes your church as it is now
Parish	The church in its community – all churches are based in a community, even if the territory is not as clearly defined as in the Church of England and the Church of Scotland

4

Roles and responsibilities

Appointments are made not in isolation but in collaboration. It is important at the outset for everyone to be clear about roles and expectations, and it is useful to ask:

- Who is responsible for which part of this?
- Who will participate in our discernment and selection process?
- Who needs to be visible and support the congregation during this time?
- Who is finally responsible for making the appointment?

To illustrate these roles and responsibilities, let us look at the Church of England. For those outside the Church of England, roles and responsibilities may have different language but understanding the tasks that each role fulfils will highlight aspects that may be useful to consider in your process.

The Church of England

The Church of England has the largest number of churches in the UK and makes the largest number of appointments each year. Every parish uses some kind of discernment and selection process, although these may differ considerably in content and style.

Vocational selection has changed dramatically in less than a generation and continues to do so. Bishops used to suggest moves to clergy, who met the parish and, if they felt there was a fit, moved to become their vicar. Sometimes this was vocational discernment; sometimes it was tactical deployment, or a combination of the two! Now posts are commonly advertised openly and suitable candidates are short-listed before several people are interviewed. This is also discernment and selection and needs to be carefully managed by all the stakeholders so that it does not become heavy-handed and competitive.

Churches will normally expect you to work with advice or support from regional or national representatives such as your regional minister, ministries council or district chair: the Church of England is different because the church representatives have to work in partnership with the archdeacon, probably the patron, and the bishop who will license and induct the minister. Although the congregation may put all their hope in the church representative as the most visible person, this is a shared process.

Some facts:

- On average, it will take at least nine months from launching the process to your new vicar preaching their first sermon.
- The vacancy process cannot start properly until your vicar has moved out of the vicarage. This is a legal requirement because at the moment the incumbent is legally in charge of the parish (freehold) until they have signed the Deed of Relinquishment.
- Each parish nominates two parish representatives to be part of the selection process. These are usually the churchwardens.
- In a multi-parish benefice each parish nominates one or two parish representatives.
- The Church of England is in transition to a new kind of working agreement for clergy; this is called common tenure. All new appointments will be made under this system so freehold will gradually disappear.

Bishop and archdeacon

Your bishop and archdeacon will have extensive experience of selecting vicars and are experts in this process. Their role is different from yours. If you look to the diocese to lead the process then you will be leaving an important part of it uncovered. You have local knowledge, while they know more about the Church of England and the regional context than you do. The strength of the process comes from drawing together your shared knowledge. Whether you are experienced in selection in the world of work or know little about it, you need to work together. Everyone has an important part to play.

We have noticed that there is often suspicion or surrender from parishes. Some feel that the hierarchy know everything and they are therefore unwilling or unable to assert any influence in the process. Others feel little accountability or responsibility to the establishment and are suspicious of any external intervention. The healthy approach, which will better serve the parish, the diocese and, in fact, the kingdom of God, is a process which is based on trust and where each stakeholder works with his or her specialist knowledge and skills to appoint the right person.

A valuable exercise for church representatives is to consider your own personal feelings on this, and those of your parish. Where are you on the spectrum between the bishop and the hierarchy having total power and the bishop just being a rubber stamp? This may help you determine whether you need to change your expectations to have a more balanced outlook.

The archdeacon normally facilitates the process. In a business setting, the archdeacon might be the HR function: the guardian of best practice who makes sure the right processes are done well. The church representative has local knowledge, and in the work setting this person would be the manager who understands the team's requirements and the context in which the individual will be required to work. The archdeacon supports the church representative to do this effectively, and may point out aspects which you haven't considered but which they see from an outside perspective and you, the insider, may miss. This may be difficult to hear, and you will need to listen and reflect when you receive challenging feedback or insights. After a painful time, one parish thought they were looking for a new vicar with drive and vision to take them forward. The archdeacon helped them to understand that what they in fact needed was someone who would work with them through the pain and restore them to become a more healthy community. Interestingly, the parish were right – and so was the archdeacon. The parish had not realized it at the time but they were describing the subsequent vicar.

It is important that you listen to and hear what the archdeacon is saying. But you have a greater and closer understanding of the parish, and sometimes you will need to balance the archdeacon's voice with what you understand the issues to be. It is a symbiotic relationship in which you input local knowledge and the archdeacon provides the context and background to the process. Both are important and need each other to make the complete jigsaw that is required for a healthy appointment.

To continue the workplace metaphor, the bishop is the chief executive, with a depth and breadth of experience and understanding of the organization and its story. The bishop is concerned for the strategy and direction of the whole organization and leaves local decisions to those with local responsibility. Sometimes there is a concern that the bishop will suggest a vicar be selected for tactical reasons, rather than an individual who will be the best person for the parish. For his own ease, the bishop will also want the appointed vicar to be right for you in your context. If this is not the case, he will need to spend an inordinate amount of time sorting out your problems over the next ten years. Therefore all parties, including the bishop, are likely to be aligned in hoping for a good fit for the parish!

The patron

The primary stakeholder in appointments in the Church of England is the patron. Historically the person on whose land, or in whose estate, the Church was built, the patron reserved the right to present the vicar for the bishop's approval. The right of patronage came with property, and it used to be possible to buy and sell it. Every Church of England parish has a patron – sometimes it is an individual or a group, a bishop, a patronage body or even an Oxford college. The Crown has many patronages, some of which have been given to the Lord Chancellor in the past. The patron's responsibility is to find and present someone to be the new parish priest. In practice, the parish still usually appoints two church representatives who act on the patron's behalf and have the power of veto. Since the vicar will be under the oversight of the bishop, he will also need to be happy with the candidate, so all stakeholders usually work closely together.

The parish representatives

The role of the parish representatives is to represent the needs of the parish within the process and to work with the archdeacon and bishop to make the right decision. Often the parish representatives are the churchwardens. Whatever happens, the parish representatives will be elected by the PCC, who may occasionally decide that others are more suitable.

The representatives can decide that there are other roles which need to be filled to support parts of the process, e.g.

- prayer lead
- editor for the profile
- data collector.

These people will work with you to help you design and deliver the clearest possible process in your search for your new vicar. It can be useful to make clear to the congregation what has been delegated and why.

Don't try to manage the process on your own. The diocese wants to support you and provides this support in different ways. In St Albans, churchwardens can get confidential personal support from the Support in Your Ministry scheme. In Oxford, the Parish Development Advisers are there to help with the audit and profile. Whether or not your diocese provides something formal, the bishop and archdeacon value the commitment and energy you are giving to the process as a volunteer. They and their administrative staff are there to support you as and when you need it.

Navigating the journey, allowing for time to offload emotionally when necessary and having a plan for what happens when things go off course, is all about sharing the burden of the process and ensuring that as parish representatives you are working together effectively to achieve the outcome.

In a multi-parish benefice, the vicar may be responsible for more than one church or parish. If so, each church is entitled to nominate two parish representatives, and you will all need to work together to create a smooth and productive process in the search for your new vicar. This will require additional energy and sensitivity, and you will need to work hard ensuring that the needs of one parish do not cancel out those of another.

Church congregations contain high emotions even when they have a leader. Church is a place where people invest themselves, and many want to feel they have influence and belong. Different traditions and even artefacts can raise anxieties and sensitivities at any time. The congregation may respond with anxiety and suspicion in the vacuum without a leader. The need to appoint a new one may result in some subtle and not so subtle lobbying. You should make yourself aware of when this is happening. Transparency is the way to counter this fear. The clearer the PCC and church community are about where and how they can appropriately influence, what they can know and why there are limits to that, the easier the process will be. Parish representatives feel the weight of the responsibility to make a good appointment: a clear process which has been communicated well and which people understand will mean one less area of stress for everyone.

Positioning may come from the best possible intentions. An individual may have a clear idea of what they feel is needed to move the parish on or maintain the status quo. They may have experience of being in a different parish where a vicar was particularly brilliant or dreadful which they feel the need to share with you. It may be only fair to listen to this out of politeness. However, having everyone bending your ear is unlikely to be an effective way of making a decision about the appointment – or of maintaining your sanity. The most articulate and loudest voices are not necessarily those that should carry the greatest weight.

Despite the risk of lobbying, the church community and PCC will be key to working with you to describe the parish and its perceived needs. Out of this you will write the parish profile and person profile, from which will come the selection criteria. Out of this in turn you will create a shortlist of potential applicants. These people will be met and a suitable candidate will be identified. And this decision will have come from the key information that the church community and PCC have identified with you at the start of the process.

There will be times in the process when people may believe you are keeping secrets from them. Sometimes that may be true. Often you will simply be waiting. It helps to be clear about what is confidential (candidates' information, decisions that have not yet been released publicly) and what is not (completed profile, timings, etc.). This needs to be clearly communicated in advance so that people understand the reasons behind their involvement in different parts of the process. Knowledge is power. It is valuable for you and your fellow parish representative(s) to be clear that you are only holding what must be confidential and are communicating what you can. For example, the parish can know that there are four people who have been invited to interview. It is not appropriate for them to know who they are.

Some people find it helpful to have thought in advance about how to respond to enquiries or lobbying. This maintains your position without being offensive or getting entangled in different people's opinions.

> Thank you for your useful input. Please can you email it to me or write it down. We will make sure that is considered at _____ alongside other thoughts.
>
>   We are not able to tell you that . . . but I am able to tell you that there have been ten applications and we have made a shortlist which fits the person profile.

> I understand you have questions and things you want to say. They will be considered at ____ and you may not hear any more about that until [x part of the process].

It is important that the names and home parishes of the unappointed candidates are known by as few people as possible, as they may not have told their current church that they are thinking about moving. After the interview day, the name of the person who has been appointed needs to be kept confidential while various administrative and logistical decisions are made by the diocese and the candidate. This may, for example, be about sorting out a spouse's job or children's schooling. In order to be transparent, the announcement of the appointment has to be made simultaneously in your church and the church from which your new vicar is coming. People talk. The kingdom of God is wider than your parish, and people know people. To take care of all those affected by this person's move, including the vicar's current parish, it is critical that confidentiality is maintained and that rumours do not precede an announcement. However, it is important to let your parish know that an appointment has been made and that you will make it public as soon as possible.

The PCC and congregation

The support of the praying church community and the PCC is vital for the parish representatives for discernment and making the right decisions.

The discernment and selection process belongs to the PCC and to the congregation. The PCC will need to

- ensure that the parish profile accurately describes the parish as it is now;
- ensure that the person profile describes who you are looking for to fill the vacancy;
- be involved in ensuring that the person selected meets these criteria.

However, it is neither appropriate nor realistic for everyone to have detailed input or control at every stage, although everyone will have an opinion! For the sake of confidentiality and fairness, some things will need to be dealt with purely by the parish representatives and the diocese. But there is a great deal that the PCC and the congregation should be involved in, especially in the early stages of the process. As well as placing responsibility within the whole congregation, this also ensures that the data which is collated for the purpose of the profile reflects fully the wider perspective of the community. It would be easy to write a parish profile which captured just the views of the parish representatives. Ensuring that everybody's perspective is considered demands more work but means that the output is truthful and accurate. An accurate parish profile is more likely to produce the right vicar – and to ensure the greatest number of people come with you!

Table 4.1 will help with an understanding of roles and responsibilities in the discernment and selection process within the Church of England.

Table 4.1 Roles and responsibilities within the Church of England process

What needs to happen	Who is responsible (usually!)
Prayer	All
Starting the process	Diocese + churchwardens (+ patron if actively involved)
Appointing parish representatives (a new role for the vacancy season)	This needs to happen by this stage in the process. Reps are appointed by the PCC and are usually, but not always, the two churchwardens
Where are we now? (Audit)	All (diocese can usefully comment)
Writing the profiles	PCC + churchwardens (consulting diocese)
Advertising	Diocese
Short-listing	Diocese + parish representatives
Designing selection process	Diocese + parish representatives
Interviewing	Diocese + parish representatives + patron
Meeting candidates	PCC + parish representatives + other stakeholders.
Prayer again	All
Decision-making	Diocese + parish representatives

Part 2

MAKING READY

5

Prayer

We are suggesting processes and activities to help you ensure that the decisions you make in appointing your new minister are as effective and appropriate as possible. This might feel uncomfortable. Is it too process-bound? Are we going to be so efficient and detailed that we miss out on the heart and soul of who the person is? Where is God in the analysis, the audit and the anxiety?

As you begin your journey of finding the right minister for your church, start with prayer. Prayer needs to be central. It needs to pre-empt the process, to weave through it and to be in the decision at the end. Prayer needs to be welcoming the new minister in and sending the old minister on their way. Prayer needs to be corporate and individual. Your style or churchmanship does not matter: this is simply about raising your concerns, hopes and fears to God and listening to the Holy Spirit. Prayer underpins discernment and good decision-making.

What prayer isn't, in this process, is an opportunity for lobbying. When intercessors raise their voices and pray with enthusiasm for the congregation to join in asking God to send an evangelical minister or a good catholic to take our church community back to its rightful place, you ought to be a little concerned. At your toddler group, when you communally pray for a minister who will take over all the children's work and do it *properly* this time, you need to be aware of what's happening. The lobbying process has begun! This is either petitioning God on personal agendas or using prayer to promote opinions to those around. Those responsible for holding the process need to be aware of this and consciously and continually ensure that it isn't happening. You want to be able to hear God guiding the church, not have someone taking the tiller and attempting to guide Him and the congregation to a particular way of thinking.

Prayer lead

Appointing a new minister is a combination of discernment and selection, and so a considered and thought-out prayer process needs to run alongside and underneath meetings and paperwork. If this is to be sustained throughout the selection process it is useful to identify an individual who will hold this responsibility. This should be someone other than the church representatives, because they have enough to do, and the responsibility of the process needs to be a shared one where it can be. It is the congregation's process, and is an opportunity for individuals to use their skills and develop their own ministry in service of the wider Church.

The prayer lead will not need to have experience of this exact role (how many people will have been in this situation before?) but have a real commitment to prayer and an ability to discern the needs of the whole community. They should be able to spot opportunities, enable prayer activities to happen and ensure continuous and valuable prayer in different ways and at times which are appropriate.

Here are some suggestions of how to do this, though you will have many more of your own which you can use. Your church will have its own style and voice and you will either want to replicate that or may want to try something a little different.

Prayer at the beginning

Be still, and know that I am God!   (Psalm 46.10)

Before you audit, consider what goes into the parish profile or get caught up in the flow of the journey to welcoming your new minister, you need to set your course. How can you enable prayer to guide the process? Where are the opportunities for corporate prayer? Is it a short prayer meeting in which prayers are offered up communally in silence? An invitation could be sent to the congregation and beyond to invite them to be involved.

Throughout the process, it is good to have an opportunity for regular prayer times: maybe Saturday morning for 15 minutes when the congregation pray at home, or Sunday before the service. Whether three or 30 attend, when you meet together praying for your church community and your future leader you are building a good foundation for a discernment process.

This prayer by Thomas Merton may be useful at the beginning of the process:

My Lord God, I have no idea where I am going. I do not see the road ahead of me. I cannot know for certain where it will end. Nor do I really know myself, and the fact that I think that I am following Your will does not mean that I am actually doing so. But I believe that the desire to please You does in fact please You. And I hope I have that desire in all that I am doing. I hope that I will never do anything apart from that desire. And I know that, if I do this, You will lead me by the right road, though I may know nothing about it. Therefore I will trust You always though I may seem to be lost and in the shadow of death. I will not fear, for You are ever with me, and You will never leave me to face my perils alone. Amen.[1]

Prayer through the process and at decision points

There will be many meetings before the decision is made and your new minister is safely installed. You could write a prayer specifically to be used at the start of each meeting, focusing hearts and minds to God's purpose. Making a commitment to using a standard prayer at the beginning of meetings is one way to ensure that prayer happens. Although you hope that it won't be sidelined, sometimes difficult meetings and critical decisions that need to be made quickly can hijack the time you have available. Giving yourselves the space and time to focus on God's desire for the community, and raising to Him your hopes and concerns, means that you will feel His presence with you at each step of the journey.

If you write your own prayer, it could be as simple as the Lord's Prayer:

Our Father in heaven,
Hallowed be your name.
Your kingdom come [in this place].
Your will be done in our church and community – and the places
 where we spend our time – as it is in heaven.
Give us today our daily bread.
Forgive us our sins as we forgive those who sin against us.
Lead us not into temptation and deliver us from evil.
For the kingdom, the power and the glory are yours,
Now and for ever,
Amen.

Open prayer is great, too. You will all have your personal preferences around prayer. Be realistic and recognize this, and make space for God to speak rather than allowing anyone to hold the floor with a list of wants and needs.

At the end of each meeting, raise the work you've done to God. Ask for guidance and support.

Prayer with the congregation

The entire congregation is not going to be involved with every decision. Yet they are critical in holding the whole process in prayer, and the wider discernment process needs to be prayed for at regular services and in small groups. How can you use other communication methods to request prayer? Examples could be pew leaflets, notice sheets, church magazines, community notice boards, websites . . . Is there a model of words that you can suggest to help the congregation to pray? Or a list of the key points that need prayer as the process unfolds? Or a timetable of the process? The prayer lead will be an effective person to plan and organize this.

Prayer can come from the diversity of the congregation: our diverse styles of prayer to God reflect our community and all are valuable. Youth groups might want to build a prayer wall where the congregation can add individual prayers. The old people's lunch club can pray together. The band can share their prayers by text. Sunday school groups might create prayer pictures. Encouraging prayer in all shapes and sizes from the whole of the church community will enable a sense of appropriate responsibility in everyone: 'The new minister will be important to me, personally. I want to make sure that God is guiding the decision-makers and that the minister applies and comes who will make a difference to our community.'

In a multi-parish benefice, where the minister has responsibility for a number of parishes, a corporate prayer process with all the parishes can be a helpful and creative part of the journey.

Prayer event

Bringing diverse prayer groups together might be an opportunity for the whole community to come together in a prayer event (more about the importance of the community later). An event, followed by some sort of food and drink, can be valuable for two reasons: praying together and building community.

One approach might be to use prayer stations.[2] Set up small displays (stations) around the building which reflect different aspects of the church and the local community as a whole. At each station there may be some words or an article to represent a specific aspect. There might be a map which covers the area at one, with some school uniforms at another, while the local newspapers may form yet another. One station may be about vision and future; another may have a torch, indicating the need to pray for the selectors and candidates as they look for the way forward.

Another idea is to have a creative prayer activity. When adults and children are given the opportunity to get messy and painty together, great things can emerge! How about using an alternative method of worship – a Taizé[3] setting, Compline or some Iona Community[4] worship – which will facilitate some reflective prayer in a communal setting?

A prayer walk around the community is a great way of bringing God into the process in a different way. This can be done silently or out loud, as individuals or in a group.

And then there is always the opportunity to finish your prayer activity off with a communal meal. A family meal, surrounded by prayer and by love – what a great kick-off for an effective process to find and appoint your new minister!

Manageable and effective prayer

We are not describing prayer-lite, but a prayer process which is manageable, fun to be involved with and effective. There will be people in your church community who are used to corporate prayer. For others, this will be new. A long prayer meeting may be right for some people but frustrating, disempowering or downright annoying for others. A managed prayer process where there is a range of brief activities throughout the discernment and selection process that suits the diversity of the community will bring people with you.

Prayer is, of course, about listening to God as well as speaking. It may be that at different steps in the process you get a niggling thought. Pray about it and talk it through with other stakeholders. It may be a niggle. It may be guidance.

Thinking is continually refocused by prayer. You give God the space which He needs to guide all the stakeholders. And encouraging prayer now also means you become a more prayerful church community as a result.

Activity

If there is a spectrum of prayerfulness, you want to make sure that you are not on the extreme that means you are so busy doing good process that you don't have time for prayer. Neither should you be on the other extreme where you just pray and wait for the ideal candidate to knock on your door. God works through prayer and action.

6

Where are you now?

With your minister gone, it may feel that you just want to get on with the new appointment rather than bothering about this process. But you need to be able to describe who you are in order to understand who you need. The question of where you are now is the essence of the parish profile from the church perspective and of the application form or ministerial profile from the candidate's perspective. To produce these documents you all need to do good preparation to ensure the data provided is actual and real. Whether you will eventually meet one person or several, whether you need copious paperwork or a paragraph, where you think you are now will help you and your new minister begin listening to God, the people and the community about your next phase.

The parish profile and the audit

It is tempting to fast forward and start writing the parish profile. A good parish profile will facilitate a simpler and more successful discernment and selection process than a profile which is inaccurate. It will:

- describe where your church is now;
- describe what the community is like;
- give an idea of where you might be heading;
- describe what kind of a minister you are therefore looking for to lead you for the next season.

You cannot begin to write it until you have done a realistic audit of where you are now. As one leader leaves and you consider the arrival of another, you have a unique opportunity to stop and take stock of where you are now. If you skip this stage, it will be like going to the supermarket without a list, knowing neither what is already in your cupboard nor how many people are coming for any of the meals needed next week.

Doing the groundwork

Groundwork can be dull. It is hard work and requires honest reflection. In the parable of the sower[1] the farmer knows the condition of his soil: rocky, dry, thorny, fertile – good and bad. He probably has some understanding of how that has happened and will know where there is no shelter, where the Leylandii trees have overgrown and made the ground dry, where the soil will hold water, and where the stones from an old wall are quite near the surface. He will know the most fertile soil for planting and whether it is time to rotate produce or let ground lie fallow for a while. Until he is honest about that, recruiting a new farmer to work with him – or handing over the farm to someone else – could mean that they will start trying to grow carrots when the soil is more suited to being a paddy field.

Your parish has a story, too. Like a farm, it will be a mixed story. Tradition, innovation, pain, hope, hard work, openness, resistance, failure and success will all be part of that story, and some of this may be difficult to accept. Honesty is important in this process. Churches which take a superficial approach to the groundwork are likely to be those which fail to appoint or where a new leader leaves quickly. This can be for several reasons:

- The profile tells a story that is superficial. You base your person profile on that and only at interview realize that you need a different kind of leader.
- You have not fully acknowledged the past. Ministers applying for your post might be willing to take on your problems and work with your secrets . . . but they will be a better leader for you and stay for longer if there is at least some transparency from the start.
- Some ministers are looking for a church which is not perfect and where there is clearly work to be done. They need to see where this is the case.

In the process of appointing a new minister, you will need to take time to think about certain questions:

- What shape is our church now – in our community?
  - demographic data
  - opinions.
- Where might we be heading?
- And therefore what kind of person do we need to take us there?

We have been told that churches should worry less about their shape and more about opening their hearts and minds to what God wants. It has been suggested that introspection like this is ungodly preening. It is not. Unless you take a realistic view of where you are now, you are doing a disservice to previous clergy and to God. It is very difficult to discern what God wants unless you can see a context for that. Clergy are a team through time. Teams comprise diverse and varied people.

You will be looking for a new minister who will lead the church in your particular context for the next season in your life. Many different stakeholders will be involved in the process. Discernment is important and begins with you and the question: 'Where are we – really – now?'

Some of the data that you discover may be unexpected. Some may be unwelcome. All the information and insights you collect will be an important part of understanding what the church is for and therefore what kind of a leader you will need next. Only then can a potential minister discern whether yours might be a church and a community where God is leading them.

To illustrate this, let's think about home improvement shows: A friend of ours was on *60 Minute Makeover*, where a couple of rooms are made beautiful by a huge team of people working for just one hour. They don't have time to pay attention to any underlying problems in the house. Our friend speaks of returning to a beautiful house, but one where you could start to see through to the old paint by bedtime, leaving an impending sense of disappointment.

On the other hand, in *The Home Show*, the presenter moves into a house for a night to live with a family and to find out what their needs are for their home, now. He listens and hears about which bits work and which areas are not fit for the purpose they need now. The family move out, everything is removed from the house including the kitchen and bathrooms, and the whole interior is sprayed white. When the family return with their life savings, the presenter discusses with them how they can reconfigure and/or extend the property in order for it to do what they need, within their budget. It's an audit of where they are now, where they are going and therefore what kind of a home they will need. Sound familiar?

In the next chapter we will offer examples of different ways in which churches have taken stock to answer the questions:

- Where are we now?
- Where is our community now?
- Where might we be going?

And in Chapter 9 we'll get to

- What kind of a leader do we need to take us there?

> Lord, show us who we are.
> Give us the courage to see ourselves as You see us.
> Shine Your light in all the corners
> So we know who we are
> And who we may be.

7

The audit

We hired our office administrator from the school playground when we needed someone to help with admin. She was another mum, organized, and we got on well. She's been with us a long time now and is the core of our team. If she were to leave we would not be able to hire the person in the playground again. Sue has developed skills as the business has grown. This time we would need someone who could already do most of the things she does. They could learn how to use our database but would already need to know how to use the accounts package. The organization has changed and developed. We wouldn't even know what they would need to do until we had first worked out what happened to get us here, where we are now and where we are going.

In order to write a really effective parish profile, you first need to spend time gathering data. In this chapter we will focus on gathering data by doing an audit in the church and community to build the information from which you will create the parish profile. We will tell some stories of how different churches have done audits to answer the questions:

- Where are we now as a church? (Church audit)
- Where is our community now? (Community audit)
- Where might we be going? (Future audit)

Whether you will be meeting people one at a time or having a more extensive interview process, self-reflection is critical before you begin.

People struggle to engage with process that actively looks at the parish because *you already know what you want your new minister to be like!* As one minister leaves – or even before – talk starts about 'what we want our new minister to be like'. One church consulted the church council about what they wanted in a new leader before the last person had even left. It's natural, and on one level it seems like the obvious question. And it is, when asked at the right time! When we did our parish audit, we directly addressed the need to describe the new minister before we did anything else. We asked the members of the church council to each write down on paper three things they wanted in the new minister. We collected all the suggestions and put them in a sealed envelope to be looked at later in the process. This cleared away the wish list and freed up time and space to do some reflection on the context. When we revisited them after the audit, there were some surprises about how much had changed!

If we had not addressed this directly, the audit process would have been tackled at a shallower level and diverted to other conversations we felt were more important – such as what we wanted our new minister to be like!

The audit needs to be a balance between data and opinion. Both are important. Dealing with perceptions and opinions is more difficult than working with defined facts and data, which are easier to marshal and understand. Even when objective data may find that a particular opinion is not based in reality, the fact that someone has a particular stance means that their view is true for them. There will be diverse opinions about where you are now and it is important that this diversity is included in the audit: every opinion is valid, even when it contradicts what others say. It can be transformational to allow people with very different opinions to all be right. For example, one group felt very strongly that the work with children and young people was one of their church's greatest strengths. Another group felt that it needed attention. Both groups were, of course, right from their own perspective and the mixture of opinions created a useful third insight.

This depth of reflection may feel quite uncomfortable to some people. If you sense resistance to doing an audit, or if your church is only willing to do a superficial audit, consider what additional insight that might give you into where the church is now.

Who to involve

Facilitator

It can be useful to find someone to facilitate the audit process. This might be someone within the church council or an independent person brought in from your congregation or community. The diocese or region will know people skilled in this area who may help you. The more independent they are, the better it will be for the process. Their role is:

- to make the process safe enough for everyone for it to work effectively;
- to ensure everyone is really allowed to be right;
- to help you to avoid getting bogged down in detail;
- to work with you to actively look for and collect themes that give you a realistic audit of where you are now.

Stakeholders

Many people will want to be involved in writing The Document! It is the church council's responsibility to produce a parish profile, and the audit is your opportunity to consult widely at the beginning of the process. Be realistic that you will not be able to accommodate everyone's wishes. Consultation and voting rights are different! In one parish where we worked, the church representatives worked hard to produce a profile without engaging with the wider stakeholders at any point. They produced a beautiful document, ready for publication, for the church council to review, and were dismayed when there were challenges and criticism so far down the line in their process. Gathering input first would have meant that it was owned by the church council. The profile would have represented how the wider congregation – and community – saw the church.

Your stakeholders may include:

- *the church council*: they usually have responsibility for the process and therefore must be engaged with the audit;
- *staff*: paid and voluntary (e.g. lay preachers, readers, etc.);
- *other church stakeholders*: your church may be connected with others in your circuit, your benefice or your team. You will need to decide early how you work together in this process and at what stage it needs to become a joint venture. Have a conversation with the other churches about how you will all collect the data you need about each church and about the benefice, and finally about how you will work together to discern what kind of a minister you will need. You will also need to agree how to pull that information together. You could give them a copy of this book.
- *patrons or trustees*;
- *regional representatives from your denomination*: archdeacon, bishop, district chair, regional minister, etc.;
- *other stakeholders in the community*;

- *other stakeholders in the congregation*: there are important people in the congregation who may not be represented on the council. Think about who they might be in your church. The person who comes Sunday by Sunday, arrives late, leaves early and never speaks to anyone; the person who is attentive and engaged in every service but not otherwise involved; those who are engaged in midweek activities and not on Sundays; and those who are beginning to wonder why they come at all.

It is valuable to keep a selection of these stakeholders in mind at every stage of the process. This may mean consulting them as well as considering them as your virtual decision-making team. At each stage of the audit, discernment and selection process, mentally consider how they would view what is being said – from their perspective. Although it is neither practical nor possible to involve everyone with every decision, viewing the process through these people's eyes as well as your own will give you valuable insights.

The focus

To start your planning, here are three questions to focus on:

Who is our church for?

Who is the church for? There is probably more disagreement in churches around this question than any other. Some think it's for the congregation, others for the community. For people like me, or for people like them. It should be for the old, the young . . . the list goes on. When a church talks about 'our church' or an individual about 'my church', it is easy to lose perspective about who the church is for. The local church belongs to much more than the church council and the minister.

- It belongs to God: 'And I tell you, you are Peter, and on this rock I will build *my* church' (Matt. 16.18, our emphasis).
- It belongs to the community. People value their local church: 72 per cent consider it an important part of their local community, 58 per cent believe it makes their neighbourhood a better place to live, and 63 per cent would be concerned if the local church was not there. Those who would be concerned include 38 per cent of people with no religion and 38 per cent of adherents of other faiths.[1]

- It belongs to the congregation – past, present and future.
- It is not simply the building. The people are the church, and they inhabit places beyond the parameters of the building: in their homes, workplaces, leisure activities and at the school gate.

What is our church for in this community?

You may already have a mission statement that says what your church is for. Is it still true? Is it clear enough for people to be able to look back at the end of the year and say, 'Yes. What I did this year contributed to what we are here for'? If not, you may need to make it more tangible.

There are many ways to engage in this process. A simple one is to ask your stakeholders to come up with three words describing what they think your church exists in the community to do: examples might be 'loving', 'caring', 'saving', 'serving', 'proclaiming', etc. Then meet up and invite them to pair up with someone else and come up with three words from their original six. You can then double the pairs into groups of four and repeat the exercise – again narrowing down to three words in total. Once people are in groups of eight you are likely to have begun to find a common mind.

Some further reflection might explore:

- If this is all we are here for, what is missing?
- Who are we here for?
- What does this mean about the way in which we are church in this community?

Where are we going?

In the Bible, John describes vision concisely when he talks, in Revelation, about a new heaven and a new earth. What will it be like when the kingdom of God is fully here? Dave Steell, a church leader, has written a vision for his community, starting:

> It was eight o'clock on Monday morning.
> I was standing by Lambeth North station.
> And I saw a new London coming down from the heavens . . .[2]

He goes on to describe what that might look like in his context. If you saw a new heaven and a new earth in your community, what would you see? In our community we would see no more loneliness, no more debt, no more self-serving, no more individualism, no more broken relationships. We would see people talking with their neighbours, sharing food, sharing money, sharing stories and sharing time.

There is something about thinking big – and of course thinking about a new heaven and a new earth in your community is both big and biblical – that allows us to see what our real passions are. It's a risk . . . but it will certainly help you be much clearer about what the church is for in the place where you are at this time in history.

Church audit

To make the most of the audit process, you will need data (facts), stories and opinions. Opinions are important, although this process is not an opportunity to lobby for particular standpoints. Clear ground rules will be needed to make it safe for people to express what they are really thinking.

Here are some ground rules you might use, which will need to be reinforced every time you meet. There will be others you will need to determine and agree as you work through the process.

- What is said here is confidential and should not be disclosed to those outside this group. This is a process and there is a danger that honest comment might be translated and represented wrongly outside of the process. The outcome of the process will be shared at the end of the audit process and will be a complete and agreed picture.
- Everyone is right: even if there is disagreement, you are both right because this is about your perceptions of how things are.
- Suspend 'what the minister must be like' until you have agreed what the parish is like now.

Data gathering: church council

You can glean opinions from the church council by bringing people together in a different setting from a normal church meeting. It's important to set the scene that this is not a committee, that there will be no voting and that everyone is right. Some parishes conduct these meetings around a meal in someone's home. The discernment and selection process needs to be a shared responsibility, even when the authority is carried by a smaller number of named individuals. It's amazing how you can change the culture of a group by meeting in a different place in different seats.

Strengths and weaknesses

We need to get away from the myth that churches are perfect places which are looking for perfect leaders. That is only setting people up to fail. It is ironic that we follow Jesus, who spent time with broken and rather chaotic people who constantly made mistakes, yet we struggle to be honest with others about our own frailties and weaknesses as churches. 'We are the body of Christ.' And like Jesus' first team, we are not all good at everything.

Think about what you are already doing as a church (or churches) in your community context and reflect together on where the strengths of your activities and involvement lie, as well as the places where you are not doing things so well.

Storytelling

Story is an important part of the Christian faith. Each week, we celebrate and retell the story of God's engagement with people from creation through to the story of Jesus and the early church. This story continues and is played out in your community every day in many different ways.

Telling the story is a command from God! Even as the Passover was about to happen, God told the Israelites to remember the story and to retell it to future generations.[3] There are stories of God at work in your community now, and perhaps you don't take the time to tell them enough. There are also stories which have influenced how your church is now. Some are good. Some are not. Whether or not people are willing to acknowledge them, the stories will appear and inform decisions consciously or subconsciously. Storytelling is not about blame or reliving the past. It is about acknowledging what has happened – even if detail is not shared with newer members of the congregation. And it's a biblical imperative! After all, we still hear the story of God rescuing the Israelites from Egypt and how they moaned pretty soon after![4]

A useful way for church council members to start the storytelling is to find out from each other in small groups:

- What brought you here?
- What connects you?
- What keeps you here?

An inner-city church in a community with a fast-moving population invited members of the congregation to bring in a photo of themselves and stick it up on a timeline around the church, indicating when they first arrived at the church. The process continued over several weeks and became a talking point among young and old.

Alternatively, you might invite people to stick up an image or a Post-it at the back of church describing a church event which has been significant to them. For some it might be losing the pews (good) or losing the pews (sad); for others, providing shelter during the floods of . . .; a baptism; having an open-air service; a minister arriving; a significant church member dying. They don't all need to be good. But they are all part of your corporate story.

You can probably think of other ways to help the congregation tell the story of the church thus far. Remember, it's about people, not just about the building. Once you have encouraged people to talk about your history and current story, it may be worth thinking about how you can celebrate that. This might be by including something in the intercessions, or having a special service of celebration or a party. For some parishes, it might be about having a healing service.

Data audit

A data audit is also useful to find out everything that is going on in the church. So, for example, in the last year, you could ask:

- How many funerals, baptisms and weddings have there been?
- What kind of church services do you offer? What is the usual attendance? Remember to include any midweek congregations and services which are led by the church at another location (e.g. care home).
- What is the demographic spread of your congregation – how many are of working age? Children? Retired?
- What else is provided by the church – groups for members and activities for the community
  - on Sundays
  - during the week
  - in the wider community?
- How many people attend?

Think of people's strengths. This would be a great task to delegate to someone who loves detail and finding out information.

PESTLE

Churches and communities are affected by what is going on in society. Think about how your parish and community might be affected over the next ten years by factors that fall into the following categories:

- Political
- Environmental
- Social
- Technological
- Legal
- Economic.

For example, how are the government spending cuts already affecting your community? And what impact will they have over the next five years? How will this affect your income? You don't have to have a plan for every community problem, but an awareness of what is happening in society and its impact in your area is an important part of taking stock.

This is a good exercise where the church council and others can generate ideas together. Start by splitting into small groups, with each group being responsible for one of these factors and recording their ideas on flip-chart paper. Once you have generated ideas for 15 minutes in groups, stick the flip-charts on the wall so that everyone can add their thoughts to the ideas already started in the small groups. Different perspectives on these factors will open up rich veins of discussion.

Outside in

After a family bereavement, we invited the local antiques man in to value the precious artefacts which were thought to be valuable but which no one in the family wanted to keep. His perception of them was very different from ours. We thought that they might be worth thousands of pounds. He wanted money to take them away!

Other people's perceptions of the church can be very different from our own. It is said that organizational culture is what you stop seeing after three months. So, however much we try and audit our own church, an outside perspective can provide fresh insights. If there is time, some of those applying to be a minister in a new parish may go and have a look first. Logistically that can be quite difficult, and although they may get a chance to look around the community, with the short notice they will get between the advert and the closing date for making an application it may be impossible to schedule in a Sunday visit. So why not do it for them?

Mystery Worshippers can be a great asset to give this outside perspective. The idea came from Ship of Fools[5] website in the 1990s. You can organize it yourself, or Church Check[6] from Christian Research will even do it for you!

Invite some volunteers to come to an ordinary service on different Sundays. Choose someone who never normally goes to church as well as someone who is familiar with what churches do – possibly with children. It is important not to brief anyone in the congregation in advance! You might ask your visitors to comment on:

- What happened as you arrived to welcome you?
- Did you feel comfortable finding somewhere to sit?
- What information were you given (in the service sheet/verbally) about when to sit or stand?
- If there was Communion, how did you know what to do?
- How comfortable did you feel in the service?
- Did you understand what was going on?
- Was there a socializing time afterwards, and what happened?
- From what you experienced, what would you say were the three key values of this congregation?
- What is their church for?

Many churches are using external measures, such as the Seven Marks of a Healthy Church[7] or Natural Church Development[8] as a valuable way of understanding the church as it is now. It might be useful to work through this as part of your auditing process.

However painful it is or however vulnerable it makes you feel, external objective feedback is an important part of answering the question **'Where are we now?'**

Taking action

The main reason for doing a church audit may be to gather evidence for the parish profile. However, along the way you may also discover that there are issues you need to address, or success and good news that needs to be communicated more widely. Take this as an opportunity for action as well as reflection.

As an example: after an exercise of taking stock, some churches started a food bank. The Trussell Trust even hit the BBC headlines for its work in responding to hidden needs in the community.[9]

Community audit

Mapping

In the Anglican Church and the Church of Scotland, parishes are geographical areas which cover the whole community. Even in a church outside any denominational system, you will have an idea of the territory which you serve. And members of your congregation are involved in the wider community during the week. There may also be parts of the parish where no one ever goes. That is useful information.

One church photocopied a street map of their parish and projected the map on to a large sheet of white paper on the wall.[10] On a couple of Sundays, they invited all the congregation to draw the journeys they regularly walked around the area and to mark buildings where they went, including their homes, with coloured stickers. They allocated different coloured stickers for different uses – home, work, voluntary work, leisure, etc.

This gave them an understanding of where the church was during the week and also the areas of the parish where no one went.

Demographic data

Demographic data is useful because it gives independent information about the shape the community is now. How many people live and work in your area? What are the major economic influences? What buildings are in your community? You can also find out what is likely to happen in the future with new build, new roads and other plans.

- What can you find out about what the community is like now?
- How is the church connecting with the community now – both inside and outside the building?
- How might it connect in the future?

Resources which might help will include

- a map of the parish;
- local council or community reports, planning applications;
- copies of local papers;

45

- tourist information;
- publicity material for public services in the parish – e.g. schools, care homes, businesses;
- if your parish church is in a business, retail, industrial or tourism area, it will be interesting to notice what times the majority of the public are around the church, and what time it is open.

You may also know about changes which are likely to impact on the community: for example, you may already know that there will be large increases in unemployment over the next five years or that a major business is moving its complete operations to the area.

What does the community really think?

If the church belongs to the community where it is located as well as to the congregation, it is good to know what the community thinks the church is for. Despite negative media publicity which sometimes surrounds the role of church in society, 72 per cent of people[11] consider the church an important part of their local community. If you can find out what the community thinks, you have some more useful data.

Consider who are the stakeholders in your community. Some will be visible. Others will not. Think about:

- local shopkeepers
- businesses
- managers of major local business/retail
- local councillors
- church hall users
- residents of elderly care home
- people in the street
- parents in the playground
- commuters
- your MP
- young people
- the person in the pub.

Think about what you would like to find out from them. Are you trying to find out what the community's needs are? Or what they think about the church? Or both?

Here are some questions you may like to ask.

From your perspective,

- What is the biggest need in this community?
- Where do you see this church involved in your community outside the building?
- Where do you go when you need space and time to think and reflect?
- Have you ever been to . . . Church?
- What is the church for?
- What could it be for?
- When did you last go?
- How likely are you to go to a church service at . . . this year?
- What would need to change for you to consider coming?

Tear Fund's Discovery programme[12] and the Faithworks Community Audit Pack[13] might be useful tools in this process.

Multi-parish benefice

As well as the suggestions above, if the minister will be responsible for more than one church or congregation and these are quite different in culture, it can be enlightening to imagine yourself in the shoes of the different groups and think about what their strengths are. This may be a real opportunity to consider the differences between the congregations as well as the similarities, and a time to celebrate both.

Future audit

Understanding where the church and community is now provides a benchmark for exploring what the future may look like. There are some facts you will have discovered through the audit process so far which are clear markers for what could come next. Much of this will be about possibility: in an ideal world, what would we be like in the future?

Questions which would be useful to explore might include:

- If *this* is what you want to be like in the future, what are the barriers to getting there?
- What activities need to happen to get you there?
- What will be difficult to change?
- What will the perception of your church be, both internally and externally?

Three useful specifics to consider are the future picture for the church

- on Sunday
- in the week
- in the community.

This broad exercise to engage with what the future might look like may also be valuable as a starting point for your vision, mission and strategy. However, resist the urge to create a formal plan at this point. If you are auditing for the purpose of gathering information for your parish profile, your new minister will be a key stakeholder in what the future will look like and will be pivotal in working with you on future planning.

When the truth is difficult to say or hear

There may be parts of the story that are painful and that you as a church have tried to suppress or avoid. Be mindful of where individuals are with your history: some may have dealt with it and for them it is no longer an issue: others may still be seething or hurt. Even long-buried issues may be raised when you go through the process. It's important to be ready for anything – whether that means you have specialists you can call on who can deal with these real issues, or an alternative process which could be brought in to deal effectively with the hurt. As a church family you need to love and care for each other: you need to have a safe environment for people to feel sad, angry and upset if required.

If your church has a history of 'doing to' clergy, you will need to decide whether that is a story you wish to be told again, or whether there is some work that you need to do before you select a new minister. Your national or regional church representatives will be able to advise you on what you might do. Some churches bring in a facilitator or interim minister to help the church process the pain before they revisit the audit and consider what kind of a leader they may need next.

The painful story is probably something that you will not want to share or discuss, and it may be something serious that has been carefully buried so as not to cause further ripples of unhappiness and despair. It has become a skeleton in your church cupboard and will become a skeleton later in your process unless you decide now how you will manage it. Candidates usually pick up when something is unsaid. It gives them a sense of disquiet. And Christians talk! It's often common knowledge that 'something happened there' and there may be more rumour than facts. One parish failed to short-list twice. During that time we had a number of conversations with people who said: 'I know something went on there but no one will tell me what it was. Did the church do something bad to the minister? I won't apply because they might do it to me.' In fact the Secret was about why the last minister had left and did not directly implicate the church. Potential candidates had to make a choice of whether to continue the discernment process. And they decided not to.

What might happen if this applies to your church? The Secret, whatever it may be, is never discussed. So when candidates start to ask questions about the history of the church, they get passed along a string of people who point the increasingly suspicious candidate to someone else to answer their question. If this happens, candidates often decide that they would rather work in a church where there is trust and openness than one where there is intrigue and secrets. Alternatively, they may be freely given a number of very different versions of what happened.

An alternative approach is to pray that the candidate will not ask difficult questions and has not heard rumours of the Secret. Once they are firmly in post, tell them that there is a history to deal with, damaged members of the congregation and significant fear. If this candidate was attracted by the picture of the world that you portrayed, are they the right person to do the necessary work to accompany them through this journey? This may not be your proudest hour but, with the full knowledge of the situation that your church is in and of what needs to be addressed, the right candidate may prayerfully be delighted to be able to use their talents and experience to walk with you. It may be that this is their vocation: without being allowed the opportunity to discern the real need, they may not see it and may take their talents elsewhere.

So how to deal with this? Have one person who is responsible for being the communicator of the Secret so that the candidates may be directed there when the question arises. Plan for what needs to be shared and what is not appropriate. For example,

- There was a child protection issue ten years ago: although many people left the church two individuals involved are still in the congregation.
- The last treasurer absconded with the church funds: she is now in prison, and as a result there is still a lack of trust within the congregation.
- The previous minister had an affair with the church council secretary: they set up home together.
- Two leaders in the church fell out and they haven't talked for three years.

These things are excruciatingly difficult to say, especially to someone you are resting your hopes on to come and be the minister you need. A strategy, agreed words and an agreed Secret Keeper will all help to get the right message across.

If you choose not to address this, the Secret may continue to damage the church and its mission in your community for years to come. It happens.

Useful tools for group work

Much of your auditing work will be in gathering ideas from a group or groups. Using a variety of tools will help you do this effectively: these might include postcards, Post-its, flip-chart paper, using sticky dots for votes.

- Collect a set of advertising postcards which are left in coffee shops, pubs, cinemas, etc. They can say anything. Spread them out on a table and invite people to choose one that represents where the church is now, or what the community thinks, or the church's greatest weakness . . . or anything. It usefully gets people away from adjectives and into concepts and emotions.
- Ideas can be written on Post-its (one idea per Post-it) and then grouped or collected into themes by small groups.
- Writing a number of ideas (one per sheet) on A4 paper is also a great way of helping a group to move round ideas and information and to prioritize them.
- If you want to sense what people are thinking without engaging them in more discussion, you can list a number of facts, themes or priorities on a flip-chart and then give each person five

sticky dots, inviting them to put dots on the ones felt most important.

If you are playing with words, a thesaurus or a verbs list[14] can help to move people along when they get stuck. Interrupting times of heavy thinking with quick-fire sessions can keep the energy flowing: e.g. a quick-fire five minutes where each person shouts out an adjective which describes the church or the church in the community.

Facilitation of the group work must be kept light and not overshadow the purpose of why you are gathered together: heavy-handed facilitation can be irritating and counter-productive. Know what you need from the meeting, and identify the most effective way of getting it.

Candidate audit

If you are a minister, rushing to complete an application form without auditing your skills first is like the parish rushing straight into writing an advert without first doing the audit or writing a profile. Your personal audit is a very important step in your process, and our advice is to start doing this before you even begin to look for a suitable vacancy. It makes what comes next easier.

How you do this will depend on your preference, but we recommend that a combination of introspection by yourself and working with a critical friend, family member or coach would be most effective.

Your personal audit needs to start in the specifics. Questions to start with are:

- In the last six months, what have I enjoyed doing? What has been rewarding?
- In the last six months, what have I done that I have been good at? How do I know?

Starting with examples is far more effective than attempting to conjure up adjectives to describe your attributes, which may be intangible and aspirational. Concentrating on what events, activities or tasks have been enjoyable and have gone well is a good starting point for this. Notice that you may not have enjoyed all the things you have done well, and that because you enjoyed something does not mean it was a success. You should be able to produce two lists, one of what has been rewarding and one of what you have done well, with some events being duplicated on both lists. Keep going until you're certain that you have exhausted all examples. This is where a second person may be helpful to keep asking the question, 'What else?'

From these lists, identify what trends there are. It may be surprising to see that your most rewarding examples are connected with leading meetings, or conducting funerals, or washing-up after the young people's party. Similarly, there will be themes which are prevalent in the examples of what went well. Now list the themes you have identified. There may be duplication again, of those which are rewarding and those you are good at. Be as specific as possible: listing 'good communication skills' is not effective in auditing what you have to offer. What is it about communicating that you are good at – and how do you know?

It is worth spending a good day on this process. The end result is that you will have a list of your gifts and talents – with evidence – which are what you bring with you to a new role. These will describe your calling and your competence to the parish: 'This is what I bring with me. Will what I have and my potential allow me to do your job in your church and community?'

Add to this list things you have enjoyed and been good at in previous roles and careers. Clarify all this before putting pen to paper on an application form. Passion in what you do (what you enjoy or find rewarding) and skill in doing it are important. By preparing in this way, you have a full audit of your skills and attributes which you are then able to compare against a person profile in order to decide whether to apply. Then you can write an effective and robust application form.

> Here, in this place, tell us what You want us to do.
> Why did you bring us here, Lord?
> What was the purpose?
> Open our eyes to see the road ahead.

8

The parish profile

Having done the planning and preparation by completing an audit of the parish to a depth which works for you (and isn't so shallow that it is without value!) you have begun to answer the questions:

- Where are we now as a church?
- Where is our community now?
- Where might we be going?

The next step is to decide what to put in the parish profile, the document which will go to potential applicants and therefore potential new ministers.

What the candidate needs

This document heralds the beginning of candidates' discernment process. They will start to explore their calling to your church by asking the question: 'This is what the church or parish or community is like – is this a place where I could be?' And by understanding how you describe yourselves as a church, candidates will start to explore chemistry: 'Could I work with these people?'

Stand in the shoes of the reader. What will they need to know by the time they have read the profile to be able to discern and decide whether to apply? The parish profile is a document which potential ministers will read first to discern whether God might possibly be calling them to your church(es) and then to decide whether to take their interest further.

Our experience is that what candidates want to know is:

- Is this place looking for someone a bit like me?
- From a brief overview, is it the kind of post I might be looking for, and would I fit the post and the house?
- What sense do I get of the kind of people in this place?
- What sense do I get of whether there is a job to be done here?
- Now that I am interested, what's the detail?

- Who wrote this, and is it a fair representation of what I will find if I get to meet them?

Avoid looking at the last profile. Your community, population and housing have probably changed since you last looked for a minister – and your church will have changed under their leadership. And don't use all the data you have acquired. It is far too much for the parish profile, yet will provide a pool from which to begin writing. You might limit yourself to themes from the audit. The rest will be useful data for the future when your new leader is in post. Bind it, save it – do what you like – but organize it and remember to pass it on to your new minister once they have been appointed (Fig. 8.1).

The mistake made by many churches is to start with what you want to say about yourselves. We recently saw a 47-page profile. It was impossible to read and began with extensive details about the location. No one wants to know about the city boundaries or the local council until they have established the basics. At this stage, just the general location is enough.

The profile is not the story of the parish, although it is in part. It is not the property details for the parish, although it is in part. It is not a description of your community, although it is in part.

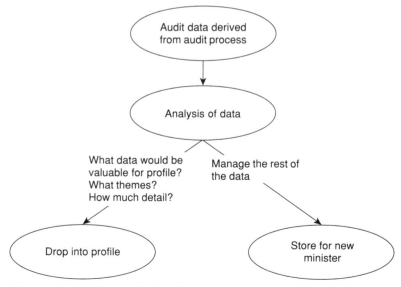

Figure 8.1 Dealing with the data

Think about films. An advertising poster tells you there is a new film out and gives an idea of whether it is a rom com or a thriller, an action adventure or an animation. You know that it will be coming to a cinema near you. And that is all. The film trailer – with the man with the very deep voice – shows clips of a few key scenes to tantalize you into watching the whole film. Or not. It does not tell you the whole story.

For churches, the advertisement or listing announces that there is a vacancy in your church – the poster. The profile gives enough key themes for a potential candidate to decide whether they want to meet you or not – the trailer. You will not find out everything about the candidate from their paperwork. And you shouldn't be expecting to tell them absolutely everything about your church in yours!

It is tempting to describe your parish in the best possible light and perhaps to air-brush some areas with which you are less comfortable. A completely formed parish and church community without need and with no apparent potential for development may not provide a role that a potential minister will find engaging. Most of the clergy we work with don't want to go to a perfect place. Even when there is plenty going on and things are going well, they would still like to go somewhere with a job to be done, where they will not just be replicating the work of the last minister. If you are looking for a leader with vision and drive to build initiatives, they may not be excited about the opportunity of a parish which is presenting itself as Practically Perfect in Every Way! However proud you are of the good works that are being done in your church, consider how this looks to the reader. They are human beings with strengths and weaknesses that they would like to bring to a church with success, potential and weaknesses. They simply want you to tell them how it really is!

Church representatives are often concerned about how the audit and profile of the not-completely-formed place will sound to the minister who has just left. Leaders come for a season, and if they are going to form the team through time, the next leader will bring different and complementary skills. Appointing a clone may look as though they didn't achieve anything much!

As well as engaging applicants with relevant information, the profile should not disengage them with irrelevant information or unintended messages. You will pick up the unsaid from the way that the candidates present themselves in their paperwork or interview. They will do the same about you! Be aware that they will be reading the words, the layout, the pictures and the gaps.

Getting it written

A camel is a horse designed by a committee. That's a warning about the risk of designing any document in a group. Having encouraged wide participation in the audit process, we recommend that the person profile is written by a smaller group of people, driven by the church representatives. At its most simple, you will need to:

1 gather the data from the audit;
2 collate it;
3 write it;
4 edit it.

Content

Make sure that your content is realistic and not prescriptive and full of your desired solutions. Remember to tell potential ministers *what might need to be done* rather than *what you want them to do and how you want them to do it.* If you give pre-cooked solutions, you risk missing a candidate who has a vision and different ideas. They need to hear from you what your challenges and ideas are and where you might be going.

We laid our profile out like this:

- one paragraph summary of the church(es)
- our new minister – five bullet-point person profile
- index
- what happens on Sundays
- midweek activities
- community stuff
- the team
- the buildings
- money and policies
- where we are now – themes, strengths and weaknesses
- possible areas for future focus
- more about the town and area.

There was a downloadable link to cover full estate agent-type details about the house, with photographs and measurements of all the rooms. An estate agent in your congregation may do a proper description for you.

Layout

The easier it is to read your profile, the more the reader will want to read on. Maybe there is important and informative information among the dense data of a 40-page profile. But the right minister may have lost patience and dismissed your church before they even find it.

Use an index so that readers can easily access what they need to find. Use a font which reflects the voice of your parish. Times Roman is seen as old-fashioned: it may suit well if your parish is very traditional, but will be confusing if your text describes the parish as innovative and visionary. Simple is best. Remember that ministers may be reading a number of profiles and will not have the time or energy to read long documents.

Writing style

You are writing this document for your potential new minister, not for yourselves. It is not Pevsner, a guide to historic buildings or a tourist information guide to your area.

Think about the voice you wish to write in. What best reflects the culture of your parish?

- chatty style (*Daily Mirror*)
- formal style, light tone (*Guardian*)
- more academic (*Times* editorial).

Whether you are being asked for a two-side summary or a slightly longer document, deciding that someone will be the editor with permission to modify the style will ensure that the profile has a consistent voice and style. They also need to be ruthless on length. This may be a different person from your detailed sub-editor, who will then check layout, grammar and spelling.

Multi-parish benefices, teams or circuits

If several churches will be sharing a minister, every church will want to have their say. Too much information or duplication will convey a clear message about your group – and possibly not the one you intend. Decide what needs to be common information, such as about the community, housing and demographics, and what needs to be separate. You will all need to be concise, and it will be a good team-building exercise for you to bring the data together. Individual parts of the profile might be written in a different voice to represent diversity, and you'll also need to pay attention to what needs to be written on behalf of the whole team, benefice or circuit – in terms of both content and style. Your reader is likely to need much less detail than you wish to give. This is where it will have been useful to have done at least some of the audit together. You will certainly need to work together to produce one person profile: you don't want to portray this role as being made up of six full-time jobs.

Colour and size

You will not need a graphic designer to make this document perfect. Remember that it will need to be accessible in electronic and paper format. Make sure that it is a sufficiently small file to be easily downloadable and, if you can, save it as a pdf file. Clergy will want to print the profiles which interest them the most. If it is too long, their excessive investment in ink may influence their impressions about you!

Pictures

Pictures of people and pictures of empty buildings will give different messages to the reader. Although your congregation, youth club or OAP lunch club may not seem to you as photogenic as your ancient church or stained glass windows, which of these you position on the front cover may send a message about whether you are people- or buildings-focused.

Editing

Our experience is that it can be difficult to edit well on a computer screen. At some point in the editing process, print out the whole document and cut it into appropriate sections. These can be laid out and rearranged with information amalgamated into themes. Once you have established a flow that works, put the cuttings in order and electronically cut and paste them to match your new text.

Ask someone who knows your context well but is not a part of it to read the profile, considering whether they think it reflects who you are now, where you are now and what kind of a leader you need next. The regional representative will have useful insights and comments at this stage.

Role description

The purpose of a role description is to make clear, both to yourselves and to your minister, what you expect them to do. Under common tenure, all clergy appointed to posts in the Church of England will need to have a role description which describes being a minister in your specific context with your challenges and opportunities. We worked with a candidate who had attended interview with his own generic understanding of what a minister's role was like. The church also had their idea of what a generic minister looked like, but unfortunately the two were not the same! If the church representatives had not made the assumption that all minister roles were the same and had instead defined what theirs looked like, the candidate would certainly not have applied and wasted his – and the church's – time.

Some denominations or dioceses will have a standard role description or a standard format. This provides a starting point to build a role description specific to the needs of your church.

The role description can come out of your audit process. In general, it needs to include:

- scope of responsibility
- accountabilities
- stakeholders
- role purpose.

Scope of responsibility

This defines the parameters of the responsibility and will list the parishes and churches in the minister's remit as well as the clergy and licensed team, church councils, buildings and church schools if appropriate. Staff who report to the minister ought to be listed here: the youth worker, the organist and the church secretary. This does not require a list of people's names, simply role titles. This section helps the candidate understand the size of the responsibility and the undertaking.

Accountabilities

This section defines tasks and accountabilities and will be produced from the work done in auditing and writing your parish profile. Split this into two categories: maintenance and development. Maintenance includes tasks and responsibilities which need to happen for the church to maintain where it is. This might include leading weekly and festival services, preaching, and leading the staff and ministry teams. Development includes those areas identified as gaps in your audit: overseeing planning and building a church housing project, developing links with inter-faith community groups, etc.

Continually keep in mind that you are describing objective tasks and not the person who will be doing them: this will come later, in the person profile. Accountabilities are tangible activities which can be observed and completed. Use consistent language to describe them, beginning with the infinitive. For example:

- To develop the ministry of lay people, through discerning talents and appropriate opportunities and giving guidance, support and training.
- To ensure that worship, preaching and pastoral care is provided for the church and community to develop discipleship and support the progression of individual faith journeys.
- To engage with residents of the new housing estate, building a presence of the church within their community.

This will enable the candidate to understand your priorities. For you, it makes clear the areas where you need the minister to be accountable. Once in post, the minister will be able to prioritize tasks and activities to meet the needs outlined in your role description, therefore ensuring that they focus on what is required.

Stakeholders

Listed under stakeholders (or key contacts) would be all of the roles with which the minister will be in contact. As well as local clergy, the regional representative and other roles within the hierarchical structure, this might include head teachers and governors, local ecumenical or inter-faith networks, and other local groups or individuals who are essential stakeholders in the role.

Role purpose

A statement which encapsulates the entire role will help the candidate's understanding and therefore discernment, as well as confirming and clarifying your vision as a church. It may be big and it may be aspirational. What, in essence, is the role of minister for? In one sentence, how could you summarize the extent of the role? Examples might be 'To be the minister of X, responsive to God's call for mission and transformation within the parish and serving the community faithfully through the seasons' or 'To be a pioneer in a location without a church building, witnessing God's love and service to the young people, families and the elderly and building a church community for worship and prayer.' If the rest of the role description is the newspaper article, this is your headline.

Write this once everything else has been completed. The broader perspective for the role purpose is derived from the audit through the parish profile to the nuts and bolts of the role description. This approach is sometimes known as 'the view from the helicopter', where the whole breadth of the role in the church can be viewed from a distance. It also describes how you are expecting this role to play its part in your team through time, so the purpose has to be beyond the present. You will need some discernment as well as wordsmithing to get this completely right, and once you have it right it will be apparent. On reading your role purpose statement, the discerning candidate may feel it resonates with them. 'That sounds like the job for me.'

This document will be used to create a person profile: instead of asking what is required of the role holder, this describes who we need to fill the role.

Candidate: application form

You will need to complete some documentation about yourself which will be much easier after you have completed your audit. This may be an application form or a stationing form. As a minister, this is your opportunity to talk about where you are now: to provide relevant data which you have clarified through your personal audit process. Simultaneously, you need to be considering:

- Might I be called to this place at this time?
- Am I competent to do the role?
- Is the chemistry between the people and me good enough?

Completing the form

This process may feel difficult, as clergy are expected to apply as if it were an external organization: maintaining a structured approach may minimize this sense. Read through all the information you are sent: person profile, parish profile and any other information that the church has felt is relevant. You may choose to do more research yourself: look on the internet, speak with the church representatives, visit the place or talk to regional representatives. Take stock of what the place needs and what it offers, and begin to think about whether your talents and needs match with what they are asking for.

Initial questions to ask yourself are:

- What might make me the right person for this role?
- What might make this church the right place for me?
- What do I need to find out *before* I submit a formal application?

Take a good look at the paperwork and what questions are asked. You will often be using a standard form, so keep in mind the requirements for the job and ensure that you are providing evidence to demonstrate your capability to meet them. The form has one purpose from your point of view, and that is to ensure that you are short-listed. Therefore you need to provide the evidence they need clearly and concisely.

Application forms ask for factual data, and that's all you need to provide. Adding in extra information about your wife's name, occupation or hobby when it is not asked for does not increase the probability of your being short-listed. Where there is a broad open question to answer on an application form, be mindful of why it is being asked. This is not your autobiography! The application form just requires evidence that is useful for the selecting church to know about you. We have seen unguarded and opinionated statements, jokey asides and academic discourses. Often application forms are also limited in space: consider that this may be for a reason! Do not be tempted to give them the whole of you, just enough for them to be able to discern whether to short-list you or not.

In brief, a good process for completing an application form would be:

1 Determine from the information provided what key themes are important to the church. The majority of this information should be in the person profile.
2 Start with who you are, from your personal audit. Review all the information you have gathered and highlight what you need to tell them that demonstrates this: skill + brief example + outcomes.
3 Produce a mock-up of the application form, particularly the longer open questions.

4 Drop key words into each of the response boxes which answer the question, connect with the needs of the church and demonstrate evidence of the talents you have identified through your personal audit. Tick them off the 'you list' as you do this.

5 Check that you have produced some evidence which relates to each element of the person profile.

6 Start writing these text boxes up in draft, ensuring that your language flows and the meaning is clear. This needs to be written in your own voice, matching the voice of the church. Remember, church representatives may not be au fait with all the language of the church and should not need a translator to understand your application!

7 Be ruthless: if you tend to be verbose, edit and re-edit until the message is clean and clear.

8 Once you are completely certain that you have provided the information that is required, produce your final draft.

9 Ask someone who you trust as a critical friend to read it through on your behalf. They need to check for spelling and grammatical errors as well as ensuring that it makes sense. Asking them to reflect what they understand about the application form is also useful: don't ask whether it describes you, as this is about you applying for this job rather than a complete potted history of yourself.

10 Make any changes, and get ready to send it off.

If the church are asking only for a CV, list the key skills you bring which fit their themes – with evidence – followed by a brief biographical list of jobs and qualifications and training.

We are often asked about covering letters. In going through the application form you may feel that there is some information that you would like the church to know but that does not seem to fit anywhere: it may be that this could be included in the covering letter. There are no rules about whether people read covering letters: in the Church of England one bishop will always expect archdeacons to read a covering letter, while another will never send the covering letter through for the short-listing process. Therefore, check what the local process is before you invest too much time and energy in crafting a covering letter.

A covering letter needs to be well written and formal, and can include the following:

- What makes you want to be their minister? (Call)
- What will make them want you? (Competence)
- If they get you, this is what it will be like. (Chemistry)

This needs to be in the application form if you are not using a covering letter. Do not duplicate information which is provided in the application form. Being clear and succinct and focusing on what the church needs to hear from you will be most effective.

Once you feel that your application form provides what is required, make sure you have a final copy saved before you send yours off by email or in the post. It is good practice to check that your application form has been received: a phone call would be a good way to do this. And then you need to hand this to God, asking for His guidance for everyone in the discernment process.

> Now to him who is able to do immeasurably more than all we ask or imagine, according to his power that is at work within us, to him be glory in the church and in Christ Jesus throughout all generations, for ever and ever! Amen. (Ephesians 3.20–21, NIV)

9

Who do you need?

The question 'Who do you need?' is answered in the person profile and is derived from the role description. It needs to do the following:

- attract ministers with the right skills and experience for your church now and in its next phase;
- help stop potential applicants from applying who would not fit;
- provide a framework against which applicants can be measured.

The person profile

The person profile needs to be precise, honed and realistic. It needs to convey the essential requirements for the new minister: this is about chemistry as well as competence. And that's it. It needs to be developed in a prayerful way. Discerning calling comes later.

A person profile is sometimes created like this: 'We'll quickly write down what we want in our new minister. Don't need to do the rest.' Then your person profile will start with five things you didn't (or did) like about your last minister and you will get applications from people who are their complete opposite (or their clone). This is likely to be unsuccessful because your last minister was the minister for that season, not for this. Therefore, the process may not result in an appointment and you'll have to start again. This will have cost you and your applicants energy, time, heartache and money.

The pertinent question to help you find the right person:

- Who do you need?

or

- Given who you are now, what kind of a leader do you need for the next season in your life?

needs to come after you are clear about:

- who you are;
- where you are now as a church;

- where your community is now;
- where you might be going.

Many churches short-circuit this and begin the process with defining who they want. The most frequent comment we receive from clergy is that churches say they want perfection. We were recently shown a person profile with almost 20 bullet points of demands in three different lists. The minister said: 'They seem to want God to do this job. There is no point in me applying.' This is a common experience, and the person profile is the document that clergy find most off-putting! Good candidates may deselect themselves on the basis of the person profile, so it must really reflect what you need.

Knowing where you are now, from the audit, will help you clarify the season your church is in. And that will help you develop the person profile. A church that needs a pioneer will become frustrated if they receive a consolidator. A church that needs loving will become frustrated if they receive a leader who travels too fast and does not take them along.

The person profile is not a detailed description of your new minister. It outlines a small number of characteristics and experiences that are essential and that you expect all the short-listed candidates to have. You will end up appointing someone who has far more than this. It is the added value that will be exciting and will lead to your decision on whom to appoint.

If you were looking to buy a house, you would create a shortlist of what was essential in a new property:

- sleeps four people;
- space for an office and wheelchair access;
- affordable;
- nice view.

This gives you the parameters that are needed to search for the right property. If you believe from the outset that, based on these criteria, the property needs to be a three-bedroomed bungalow with an office extension overlooking a field, with a white bathroom and a pine kitchen, you are restricting your options. You are establishing the answer before having really explored what might be the potential alternatives. In fact, an apartment with sufficient bedrooms and lift access, combined with renting local office space, might be an equally good solution. Like the housing shortlist, the person profile creates enough parameters to understand what is required, but not so many that it will restrict who you will look at.

Defining the person profile for your minister is like establishing the shape of the missing piece in a jigsaw. It makes the search simpler. Once you have something that only includes the essentials, it will be easier to draft an advert or short statement that will attract the general shape of applicant you are interested in. The shortlists can be based on that. The selection criteria will be driven by it. Interview questions will be formed from it. All being well, the appointment will be made with it in mind, although people will also have different added value and calling.

O God, thou art my God; early will I seek thee.   (Psalm 63.1, KJV)

10

Considering your next minister

Person profiles will often tell an unintended story about your church. There seem to be three broad types of person profile that are written, and they say as much about the people who wrote them as they do about the church!

1 *Gabriel* An Angel Gabriel profile is written by a church that wants perfection. You dot all the 'i's and cross all the 't's to make sure that you get everything in . . . and your list becomes both perfect and unattainable:

- good communication skills
- good sense of humour
- good with children and young people
- person of prayer
- excellent leader
- understands planning laws (may have been trained as an architect)
- outstanding preacher and teacher . . .

    And the list goes on. Remember that your new minister will be human and flawed, just as you and the parish are. No one will be perfect.

2 *Clone* You loved your last minister so much that your profile describes them. You may still be grieving your loss. But is that actually who you need for the next season? If they did a good job, the kind of person you need for the next stage of your journey will be different. Even if you are happy with the way the church is working, a change of leader may require a different combination of skills, gifts and interests.

3 *Inverse* We play a game with churches where they give us their person profile and we tell them what their last minister was like. It can be scarily true. The first five points on the person profile are usually the opposite of your last minister. Then the next few are just like them because you remember that they weren't so bad after all. It may be that the right person to lead you forward is the opposite

of the last person. But that needs to come from a good audit of where you are now, and not from an unconscious kick-back.

One application pack included the person profile after more than 30 pages of detail about the history of the area, the ornate carvings around the font, and the floor plan of the rectory; eventually there were three ambiguous lines dedicated to the person profile. It felt as though the minister was pretty irrelevant, after all the great things that were said about the buildings. Were they looking for a leader? Or a curator?

Planning process: the jigsaw

To explore further the essential shape of the minister you are looking for, think about the metaphor of a jigsaw. Finding out who you are helps you see the picture on your jigsaw: from your audit, you have identified together that you are 'A Day Out at the Fairground' rather than 'Tranquillity over Lake Como'. Now that you are all in agreement about that, you can begin to move to the next stage.

This is about discerning what colour and shaped piece is required to complete the puzzle. Without a really clear idea of which jigsaw piece you need to complete the puzzle – the sky, an edge possibly – the following scenario might well happen at the selection wash-up:

> *Church rep 1*: I liked our first candidate. I liked how red he was and how he wasn't the standard shape.
> *Church rep 2*: Really? But the second candidate was a corner. I think corners are good. Safe, strong . . . just what's needed.
> *Archdeacon*: Hmmm. I think candidate four was a piece of sky. That would be great in this place.

Without defining both the *context* and the *shape* that you are looking for, decision-making becomes problematic and random. Individuals will be assessed only on the basis of what they say on paper and in person, not on whether they fit your context. Working out the shape of the role you need filled gives you the general outline of the person you will need. Then the evidence brought by the candidates, their description of who they are (a large orange piece with a flat bottom, possibly), can be considered to see if it fits the hole. And we're not looking for a perfect fit – just one that is good enough – as the new minister will grow and develop into the role as they get to know you and your community. Unlike a real physical jigsaw, it's possible to have a piece that nearly fits because, if there is a gap, we can check to see if there's anyone else who has the necessary skills (whether that is sorting the finances or leading the school assemblies).

The shape of the jigsaw is about competence and chemistry. You need candidates who are able to do what you need, and will fit with those they need to. In another church, the candidate's competence and chemistry would work differently: there they may be a piece of the ocean whereas here you see them as part of the sky. The metaphor describes why it's important to get this right.

Seasons

You want to find the person who is called to be your next minister. You want to be able to hand the church over to someone who will be able to run the youth group, manage the enthusiastic team of volunteers, be an inspirational spiritual leader, lead high-energy – and deeply reflective – worship, as well as sort the administration and look after the disintegrating fabric of the church building. Or do you? This is a time for discerning what specific attributes are critical to *your* context *at this time* rather than developing an unrealistic wish list which will encourage good applicants to deselect themselves.

Just as there are seasons in life, the church goes through seasons. It is beneficial to be clear about which season the church is in now and to explore the essential characteristics of someone who will work in this season as it moves to the next (Table 10.1). The new leader needs to be able to maintain what needs to be maintained, make changes with you and keep it safe enough for you to be willing to travel with them.

Reality

Think about Jesus' team. None of them would have been able to apply for any posts advertised in the church press or in vacancy lists in the twenty-first century. They have insufficient academic training. They are not all great team players. Simon Peter can fly off the handle; James and John are more interested in self-promotion than working with other people. Matthew has a dodgy business background.

Table 10.1 Seasons in the church's life

Season	Church	Leader
Spring	• Looking to the future about how it is operating • Sense of possibility as yet unrealized • Can follow winter if the church is coming out of a difficult time	• Gentle • With vision • Strategic • Needs to be able to nurture tender ideas/people • Allow time for growth
Summer	• Performing • Lots going on • Things going well • Confident • Achieving	• Able to keep everything running – maintenance • Spot new opportunities • 'Chief Executive' who will oversee what's going on – whether staff or congregation volunteers
Autumn	• Needs tidying up/pruning • Some things may be overgrown • Some things may have reached their natural end • Energy may be going into things that need to end	• Consolidate • Prune • Reassess with you where the church is • Clear away and begin to develop a vision for the next season
Winter	• Waiting • Some may find cosy winter cold comforting and not want to get out in the spring • If there is a need to change, may be looking for someone else to take responsibility	• Giving people love and attention • Supporting, comforting • Holding the process as the first signs of spring emerge • Waiting

Does God demand perfection or brokenness? Do you require perfection from your new minister? Your new minister will be, as you are, a work in progress who will be striving to do God's work but who will be flawed and make mistakes. They will be an ordinary person – like the people Jesus recruited. It may seem tempting to try to appoint the completed person, the one who no longer needs to learn or change and who has all the answers, but they may not give your church what it needs now. St Paul is very clear that it is community that we work with, and that different individuals will bring different gifts:

> Are all apostles? Are all prophets? Are all teachers? Do all work mira-
> cles? Do all have gifts of healing? Do all speak in tongues? Do all
> interpret? (1 Cor. 12.29–30, NIV)

If your new minister is an expert in every area, there will be less need for others to step up and develop their ministry. Your minister is not your church. On their first Sunday, one minister stood up and said: 'I'm not perfect and we're in this together!' That openness and honesty allowed people to engage more deeply and feel that they also had permission to fail.

> There is a shape that we need to fill.
> Help us to identify the lines.
> Guide us in our thinking
> So we can draw confidently
> In the knowledge that our design
> Is Your design.

11

The person profile

Clarity

We saw a document which included three separate person profiles and where tasks were confused with attributes. It was impossible for candidates to be either clear or concise in communicating what they might bring to the role: their responses could only be as verbose and confusing as the profile itself. As a result, the church may well not have short-listed the candidates who were most likely to be called and competent for that role.

The clearer you are in your person profile, the clearer the candidates can be, making it easier for you to discern whether they might have the calling, competence and chemistry required.

Five bullet points are a good benchmark for the person profile. The more you include, the less likely you are to find someone who matches your profile. This means ruthless prioritizing. You will need to discard all the elements which are not essential for the job.

There are a number of ways to write a person profile effectively: we recommend you use some of the ideas from each of these sections.

Start in the fantasy

If you feel that you are becoming unrealistic about your new minister, it can be valuable and cathartic to start by brainstorming all the attributes and skills you would like your new minister to possess. Flip-charting under the heading 'In our dreamy ideal world, we want our new minister to be practically perfect in every way, and this includes . . .', or something similar, means you are continually mindful that this is not a real list. Once you have spoken all your expectations out loud, you will then be able to see that they are unrealistic and begin to prioritize exactly what *is* required in a minister to meet the needs of your parish.

Themes

This is where all the work on the parish profile and audit will start to bear fruit. Now that you have established what the church is like, it should become clear what competence and chemistry your new minister will need. Demonstrating a clear link between the needs of the parish now and what you require from your new minister will help you in ensuring that what goes into the profile is the important stuff.

The flow should therefore look like Figure 11.1.

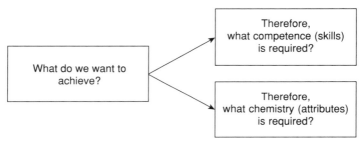

Figure 11.1 Purposeful planning

You may have identified key tasks when determining where you are now: for example, in the next year you need to start plans for building a new church hall. Identify the competence required to make that happen: an ability to build an effective team; inspirational leadership to engage congregation and community; project management abilities – all these may flow from this. What chemistry is required: a negotiator, a mediator, a networker?

If you've identified that there is a large old people's home being built, is it important that your minister has experience of ministry with older people? You have identified that there will be a considerable shortfall in your funding: does your new minister need to have evidence of addressing and turning around financial issues? Or the ability to make connections with people and get things done? You have realized that some of the worship has become stale and is not communicating with the diversity of people within the area: does your new minister need to be excited by the potential of fresh expressions of worship?

Person profiles are written for jobs in the commercial world, too. There it is best practice to be clear of the link between

- *What* is required to be done (tasks/job accountabilities/competence); and
- *Who* is right to do it (chemistry).

In that world governed by employment law, it is important to be able to prove that the attributes you require are driven by the role description. Although churches don't have to adhere to the letter of the law here, best practice will ensure that the person profile you write is fair and does not include unnecessary demands. You can only make gender an issue in the profile if you are an Anglican Church which has adopted Resolutions A and B.

Ask the church council

Invite each person to write down three skills (competence) or attributes (chemistry) which they consider to be essential for your new minister in your context, excluding generic skills of a minister.

Then ask small groups to come up with ten essentials in total. Write down these top ten on small index cards, with one essential on each card. Be specific: 'leader' is not useful. If a specific kind of leader is required – for example, a collaborative leader – record that. Rank these ten first on gut feel. Now take the tenth card away and fully consider that loss. Take your time here. Repeat until you are left with only one key essential. Then take that away.

This is the time to be realistic. Bring the most important theme back in and then progressively the others. Are they really essential? Would someone who did not have that be totally unable to be your new leader? Or is that aspect only desirable?

Analyse

Once you have established your key themes, they will need greater analysis. Be clear on the part that the minister plays in the process to make them happen:

- Is it a doer that's required?
- A facilitator?
- An enabler?
- A leader or a manager?
- Does the minister need to be able to discern talent and use it effectively? There is a huge difference between someone who is able to use willing volunteers well and someone who can find great

volunteers from a community where it appears there are no people able to volunteer.

Consider what the responsibility of the minister is within each area. Using a table like Table 11.1 to determine this might be helpful.

Table 11.1 Analysing the minister's responsibilities

	Do	*Facilitate*	*Lead*	*Manage*	*Spot talent*
Services	✓				✓
Outreach		✓	✓		
Children's work				✓	✓
Teaching	✓				
Stewardship					✓

A minister was not talented at working with young people or creating all-age worship but was excellent at spotting, encouraging and developing potential volunteers to work in groups and to lead outstanding family services. The person profile said: 'Good with children and young people'. Are their skills enough? You will probably want the minister in the main service on a Sunday and not with the young people, anyway!

Once you have determined what skills are required in each of the main areas you have identified, use the same grid to mark on what is essential and what is desirable. This calls for some ruthlessness. The important question is: in all honesty, what cannot be done without?

Start with broad themes. Do not wordsmith until you are clear that you have established the correct areas to focus on.

Content

If you are aiming to keep to five bullet points:

- *Know what to assume* If you are looking at buying a new car, you would assume that you'd want one with wheels and brakes, and therefore these would not form part of your criteria. It can be assumed that the applicant can write and deliver sermons. If one of your priorities is that the individual can 'communicate the gospel clearly, sensitively and imaginatively', that is an attribute that needs to be in the person profile.
- *Is this criterion really about the candidate?* Some person profiles state that a good sense of humour is essential – often followed by

an exclamation mark! This says more about how the parish wants to describe itself than being a requirement for the next minister. It is similar to the statement 'You don't have to be mad to work here ... but if you are it helps!' If you need applicants to be personable, with the ability to communicate and interact with a variety of individuals, then say so. Alternatively, if you want a minister who can double up as the clown at children's parties, that will also need to be made clear.

- *Ensure that the bullet points make sense* 'Good communicator' means little when we consider what a range of options this covers: the skills required by a cold-calling sales rep, a chat-show host, a hostage negotiator, a technical writer and a dog trainer could all be described as good communication skills, but the communication skills required by one are not those necessarily required by another. If by 'communication' you mean interpreting the gospel appropriately in your context, say so. There are some stock phrases that we see regularly in job adverts – 'good communication', 'team player', 'dynamic' – which need explaining to be meaningful in the person profile.

- *Consider how to measure the candidate against these criteria* Start considering this before you get to the meeting, so that the process of selection is more effective. Describing something in the person profile which cannot be measured is not particularly useful. How would you measure 'passion for practical, hospitable Christianity?' What sort of evidence would convince you of the minister's suitability? Conversely, what would convince you that they did not match this requirement? Evidence will come from a range of sources both formal and informal: self-reported data (paperwork and interview),[1] observable data (audition and interview) and external data (references).

- *Get other perspectives* You have the inside track on what your church is like. It's good to get an outsider's impressions, both of what others see in your church and of the three key things they think you need to look for in a new leader. Ask other stakeholders, including regional representatives. Their perspective will shed some interesting light.

If yours is a multi-parish benefice or more than one church is involved in this process, remember prayerfulness and humility are key. You can do the prioritizing exercise together. Each church could come up with their top ten and then you could work together to prioritize, rather than each writing individual person profiles. Think of how tricky negotiations are successfully navigated. All parties enter the negotiation with their own point of view, are clear what the deal-breakers are and then negotiate with give and take to come to a decision.

In the end you will come up with about five short and clearly written statements describing the essential criteria for the minister you need to lead your church. Challenge these. Ensure that they make sense and fit with your church's needs for the next season. This part of the process is now over: you have invested the requisite time and energy which will have helped the whole process of discernment.

Allow time and prayer

Working through this process may feel rigid and formulaic. Make sure that time and space for prayer, thinking and reflection are built in. As you collect themes about what your new minister needs to be like, take a few days to mull and reflect before narrowing them down. Timing is important. Don't rush this part of the process. You will be living with this person for many years to come!

> Then I heard the voice of the Lord saying, 'Whom shall I send, and who will go for us?' And I said, 'Here am I; send me!'   (Isa. 6.8)

Part 3

DISCERNMENT AND SELECTION

12

How do you do it?

The question is now more than: 'Who do you need?' We now need to ask: 'How do we find them? How do we do it?'

> It was he [Christ] who gave some to be apostles, some to be prophets, some to be evangelists, and some to be pastors and teachers, to prepare God's people for works of service, so that the body of Christ may be built up until we all reach unity in the faith and in the knowledge of the Son of God and become mature, attaining to the whole measure of the fulness of Christ. (Eph. 4.11–13, NIV)

Paul assures us that there are different roles for different individuals, and that together we can build up the church. So we need to be certain that our method in selection will provide us with the candidate who will enable the building up. We need to be able to find the person with calling, competence and chemistry.

Once you have identified who you are as a community and what you need, considering how you go about getting the right person is critical. This is about discernment and selection: measuring evidence provided by the candidate against the needs identified, listening to God for guidance, and measuring what you observe as well as what you read and hear.

The discernment process

Discernment and selection do not exist in isolation from each other. Time must be set aside and protected within the selection process to allow for prayer and listening. So the fact that this book has separate sections on discernment and selection does not mean that they operate independently. They are interwoven, and you will need to pay attention to each in a different way.

How does God normally guide you?

Aside from head and heart decision-making, how do you determine when God is guiding you and when it is bias or gut instinct which is informing your decisions? Some people are clear and certain of how God speaks to them. Most do not have such clarity and may see God's actions and guidance only much later, with the benefit of hindsight. God speaks to people in many different ways. Spend some time considering how and where God has spoken to you in the past so that you are more able to recognize His guidance again.

Rooting the process in prayer in a regular and formal manner is the cornerstone of discernment: prayers for guidance, both individually and so that you can corporately discern the will of God in your community, and prayers when you are sitting together with the pile of forms in front of you for short-listing. This is all about opening up to hear God and being ready and aware to listen to Him. Some of you will discern during quiet reflection after you have read forms or met people. This raises an interesting question about pace and whether candidates should be told on the day whether you are offering them the role or whether you need a little more reflection time first.

Different people discern in different ways, and you will need to come up with a common language which allows every stakeholder to be clear about what they need to communicate.

The trust between the church representatives and other stakeholders is invaluable here: deep conversations require trust which will build exponentially as you are honest with each other. 'I feel very strongly that God is telling me to consider *this* applicant. I don't know why because the application doesn't look that strong. Does anyone else feel like this too?' may lead to a useful discussion. So might: 'I am wondering whether . . .' Possibly someone else may be feeling exactly the same. Conversely, others may be surprised, and then it is useful to explore further why you feel like this.

Everything within the discernment and selection process needs to have a purpose. You need enough evidence to enable a decision to be made. The church needs enough evidence about the candidate to make a robust decision. The candidate needs enough evidence about the church and the community to make a robust decision. It is not sufficient to use interview questions which you have read in a book, or the same process as your neighbouring church used last year. In order to make decisions about your church, now, the process needs to be designed specifically to dig out the evidence that is required in your context at this time.

The temptation may be to start designing interview questions rather than following the process through. The mind immediately shifts to 'Tell me about your strengths' and other stock questions. In fact, every interview process is unique to its context, and paying attention to making this encounter fit for purpose will aid the discernment and selection process for everyone.

What is the purpose of meeting the candidates?

For the candidates, the selection process will be a time to see the parish and to meet the key stakeholders in the life of the church, to ask questions, to get a sense of whether there is a job to be done and to explore whether this might be a place where God is calling them. This is about familiarization, conversation and discernment.

For the church and other stakeholders, the process is an opportunity to find out whether what the candidates say about themselves on paper matches what you experience at first meeting. It's an opportunity to see the candidates in action, to find out more about them and to discern whether God might be calling them to be your next leader.

Exploring calling, competence and chemistry means that it is possible to hold a creative tension between conversation, observation and selection, but you will need to pay the balance some attention. You should be able to discover the data that you need without putting the candidates under so much pressure that they become actors and you don't meet the real them. And the process needs to be more rigorous than a cosy chat, because an interview is not a normal conversation. The hope is that you can both gain the evidence you need around competence and chemistry and have a quality dialogue which allows the interviewers and the candidate to explore the calling question together: the minister's calling and the church's calling. Dialogue is about understanding and learning. It is not about judging, weighing and making decisions. That is what happens after the candidate has left the room. So, in your planning, you will need to ensure that there will be enough time in the interviews to ask the questions that you need to gain evidence and to have the higher-level conversation that is true dialogue, where candidate and interviewers can think together. We are aware that this is a tall order for a group which is only formed for the day. If you strive towards this, you will be working in service of the church, the candidate and God.

What are you trying to achieve?

There is a range of information that will be used to assist you in your decision-making process. This may include what is provided in interview and audition, the application form that is submitted, the covering letter and any additional information that the candidate has decided to include for you.

So your approach to the evidence that is offered needs to be considered. Without a clear understanding of what you are looking for, it may be that one piece of data will be given undue significance and therefore skew the rest of the process, with the result that you may miss the most appropriate candidate.

You may choose to think about these questions:

- Is this candidate called to be here?
- Are they competent enough?
- Is the chemistry right?

Selection is about probability: you are trying to establish the probability of this person being effective in your role, and this works on the assumption that previous experience may indicate whether they will fit into your context.

A robust discernment and selection process

Following a robust process will enable you to see all the information you need at this point. Being analytical and allowing room for discussion, challenge and, critically, guidance from God puts you in the best position to be able to short-list and make right decisions.

> In the detail, in the minute iterations and considerations,
> Lord, be with us.
> In the process, in its formality and structure,
> Lord, be with us.
> In the decision, and the potential that will be realized,
> Lord, be with us.

13

Preparing for the process

The process that you have followed so far is important, and you have already discerned answers to two questions:

- What shape are we as a church in our community?
- What key skills (competence) and attributes (chemistry) does our new minister need to lead us into the next season?

Focus shifts now to the discernment and selection processes: how you prepare for these is covered in this chapter.

Letting the world know

Once the person profile has been completed, you are in a position to announce to the world that you are looking for a new minister, and the discernment process for you and the candidates can begin in earnest.

Every year, about 550 clergy in the Church of England move posts. In the Methodist Church, about 130 are stationed. Even more think about whether it's time to move. If you love your home and are selling it, you would prefer the purchaser to be someone you would like to live in your house. There will also be a few people who view it who you would rather not be the purchaser. But the more viewings you have, the wider the pool of potential buyers. It's the same with advertising your vacancy. You want to raise interest in your church, which will give you a wider pool of candidates so that together you can discern who is the right person to be your next leader. God is part of the discernment process, but if the person God is calling to be your next minister is unaware you have a vacancy, they won't apply!

A standard method is to advertise or to post the vacancy in appropriate magazines or church press. But there are other ways too. The list below is not exhaustive but will help you identify more creative ways of making the vacancy known which are appropriate to your church and context.

The regional representatives

Regional representatives will probably tell clergy they meet about your post, and may encourage those who might make a good fit to apply. Clergy may receive mailings from their regional office which include advertisements. The regional office may also list advertisements on its website. And you can list it on yours. Relying just on the regional representatives means that the pool of applicants may be fairly small: communicating news of the vacancy nationally is also important.

Central office

Ensure that central operations are aware and are communicating the vacancy: in the Church of England this would be the role of the Clergy Appointments Adviser, who can display the vacancy on the website. Methodist vacancies are listed centrally. Baptist jobs are placed on the Pastoral Vacancy List.

Formal networks

Formal networks might also list your vacancy, such as the Society of Catholic Priests, CPAS, New Wine. It may be that the patron (in the Church of England) or the regional representative can provide you with an appropriate list of where to post your vacancy.

Search

Some churches launch a formal search process. Informally, the grapevine may be useful. Letting the right people know (Malcolm Gladwell calls these 'connectors'[1]) can be a cost-effective method of getting the word out. Social networking is also effective: do not necessarily use the network which is your preference for catching up with friends. Ensure that the medium you use is one that is appropriate for your purpose.

While some of these methods are free, others cost, so ensure if you choose to place an advert that it absolutely does what you require. Your regional representative should be able to help you with this to ensure you are not wasting your money.

Advertisements

Advertisements can be posted in various publications, e.g. *Church Times*, *Church of England Newspaper*, *Life and Work*. Advertising can be costly but has a wide reach. There are websites which provide free advertising: however, the appealing value of this needs to be balanced against how many hits are achieved.

The space for Methodist churches in the stationing handbook is short enough that it can be treated as an advert. If you decide to advertise, your advertisement must come out of the parish profile, person profile and role description. All your honesty in the process thus far needs to continue through the advertising process: an air-brushed advert which asks for the Angel Gabriel with a smile will not attract anyone.

Communicate both the key responsibilities of the role and who you require to do it. Make it appealing. You would like to have as many suitable applicants interested and excited by the opportunity as possible. The wording of your advert needs to describe your church and be distinctive enough to say more than that there is a vacancy for a minister in Liverpool.

One parish were looking for a particular type of minister and used unconventional language to describe the role. This was effective, as more traditional candidates deselected themselves right from the start and only those attracted by unconventional language made contact.

Whatever medium you use, the more effective your advertising, the wider your pool of appropriate candidates.

Designing a good process

Having defined clearly what you need in your new minister, maintain the hard work and make the most of it in the discernment and selection process. Be careful, because it's easy to stop focusing on the person profile and start thinking what questions need to be asked or how you might show the place to the candidates. This is akin to getting detailed drawings for the extension to your house and then not refer-ring to them once the builders arrive.

From your perspective, the important questions around how the selection process works are:

- What do we know already?
- What do we need to know by the end of the process that we don't know now?

- Where will we find this?
- How will we process what we have found and how will we make a decision?

Therefore, consider your **selection strategy**. You have already written your person profile – essential and desirable competence and chemistry. The question is how to find out whether a candidate has sufficient elements of your list to be your minister in this place at this time. This is the selection strategy: without going into the detail of the exact words to use at the interview, you will need an overall picture of how the evidence is going to be gained and must accompany that with a discernment process about calling. We are aware that you might be uncomfortable with the phrase 'selection strategy'. Call it what you like. Whether you meet one or ten people, what is important is that you do it.

As well as giving yourself the data required to make a good selection decision, setting a strategy also gives you more of an opportunity to reduce any lingering personal bias. Past experiences feed expectations: therefore, without you being conscious that they are doing so, good and bad experiences of ministers in the past who may have spoken a certain way, been of a certain age or have come from a certain college can haunt proceedings. It's unhelpful: often the summary assumptions that we make are ill-founded and lazy in essence. That's not to say that 'gut feel' has no space in this process, but it must not be the driving or guiding force.

The selection strategy should come out of collaborative discussion and should cover:

- What do we want from this process?
- What needs to be in the process and why?
- Who should be present at what stage?
- Who takes responsibility for what and how will they know?
- What data are we looking for? And what will we do with it?
- How will we make our decision? What will we do if we don't agree?
- What numbers of candidates do we expect at each stage?

The selection process will clarify the unity of purpose. Nerves from different stakeholders in the process can easily skew it into something that it was not meant to be.

A level playing field

Ensure that there is fairness in this process. Consider carefully what evidence you use: the playing field is not level if you are using additional information about some candidates only. For example, find out whether all applicants have online profiles with recorded sermons before you start listening to one. Whether the one you listen to is brilliant or dreadful, you will know more about this candidate than about those who do not have an online profile. That begins an inequality. Investigate what evidence all applicants may provide before doing anything with it.

If the process is not going to be a level playing field, do not describe it as a fair process. If there is an internal candidate who looks right for the job and you are just going through the motions of a process, is it fair to suggest that all other candidates have an equal chance?

Paperwork

The regional representatives should be able to advise you on the appropriate paperwork or application form to use. Some Church of England dioceses may use one format for all their clergy vacancies, but there is often some variation. If you can choose, consider what information you need to receive from the form.

Think about what else should be sent out to candidates requesting application forms. As well as the application form, parish profile and person profile, there may be other useful documents to include which provide more information on the context. Do not overload the candidate: anything else included should be considered only for its merit, and a list of appropriate websites in the covering letter might be sufficient. Many churches or regional representatives will also email the application form so that it can be completed electronically.

Timing

Identify proposed timescales early on. Be realistic so that you can give the process the appropriate attention. These timelines will change, but a plan that is agreed from the outset will help drive the process forward. Timelines may be instigated and driven by the regional representatives and their diaries. This will need to be balanced against

Table 13.1 The selection time plan

What	When	Who is responsible
Advert placed/stationing communication		Regional rep/church reps
Deadline for applications	+ 3 weeks	Candidates
Shortlist	+ 1 week	Regional rep/church reps
Request references + invite for selection	+ 1 week	Usually regional representative
Selection event	+ 3 weeks	Regional rep/church reps + others
Decision made		Regional rep/church reps
Communication to candidates		Regional rep/church reps
Feedback from regional representative		
Appointment made	+ 1 week	Regional rep/church reps
Arrive in post	+ 3 months	Regional rep/church reps

the sense of urgency: both you and the congregation will be eager to bring the new minister in as quickly as possible!

Depending on how your selection process is structured, your plan may look something like Table 13.1.

The dates of appointment and licensing/induction will depend on the notice that needs to be given in the new minister's current post. For the purposes of Table 13.1, general dates have been given which are generated by the previous event. Once you can set an induction date which seems real and achievable then the process becomes exciting and energizing.

Receiving applications

Many factors will determine the number (and quality) of applications that are received, so predicting the response will be difficult. It might depend on other jobs being listed at the same time. Few jobs are advertised over the summer or around the major festivals such as Christmas and Easter. You may have decided that you would like to receive ten applications or enquiries from which you will short-list four or meet one. This is useful as guidance but do not use it as an absolute measure of success. There is a limit to how much you can control: a well-written and exciting advert may have little response if other churches in the area have well-written and exciting adverts – and a beautiful house as well!

If you are involved in a one-at-a-time process you will not have to work through this level of detail, but a strategy is still important.

Before you begin

A note on confidentiality

Confidentiality in the process is vital. You have a duty of care to protect the candidates and maintain the integrity of the process. Establish from the outset who will be given access to information and why they need to know this. All stakeholders need to be told about the importance of confidentiality: names must not be discussed outside those who are allowed to know (usually the church representatives). Later, perhaps when the church council need to be involved, they also must understand the significance of confidentiality. The candidate may well not have informed her church that she is looking for another job: unintentionally, information can be passed from person to person – 'I saw your minister the other day: she was at our selection day. Seemed really nice' – and the candidate finds herself in an awkward and possibly vulnerable position in her current post. Limit the number of people given access to information, ensure the significance of confidentiality is understood and do not use candidates' names.

Bias and emotion

You will want to meet the right person for this role. How do you discern whether what you are doing is based on evidence, guidance or prejudice – positive or negative?

Before you dive into reading applications, we want to give you some warnings about what might happen next. This may be the first time that you have had contact with the candidates, and from now until decision-making you need to balance facts, feelings and discernment. It will be important to recognize when you are making a decision based on hard evidence that you have been given, and when your decision is based on feelings. You need to be mindful of your natural bias and your emotional response.

The 'halo and horns effect' is a **cognitive bias** where you make a decision rapidly, based on very little information. You might use a gut instinct to make a general assumption about the candidate. A candidate greets you at interview by extending her hand, giving a warm smile and a firm handshake. From this one piece of evidence you assume that she is confident and successful – the 'halo effect'. If a candidate avoids eye contact and mutters a greeting, and you decide that he is insular and uncomfortable communicating with people and generate a negative impression of him, this is the 'horns effect'. One trait from a first impression makes us infer a general assumption which is a vast over-simplification and may well not be true.

Years ago, one of us interviewed a candidate who was the spitting image of someone they knew well and did not particularly like. This had to be acknowledged in the decision-making process and other stakeholders allowed to have a greater influence on the decision. It is difficult to be listening properly when someone seems to appear from your past!

Humans like to believe that we are right, particularly in our ability to understand other people. When we are supporting people in recruiting, it is dispiriting to be told, 'My gut instinct about people has never let me down.' Actually it tends to be the ability for self-delusion which is the let-down. Coupled with the halo and horns effect our tendency for **confirmatory bias** is another inclination which can mask our ability to assess effectively and from evidence. Once you have decided on a first impression that the individual is confident or intelligent, you then search for evidence to support this conclusion. This is hard work for the interviewer: listening out for evidence that will confirm the initial decision and overlooking evidence that is contradictory. At the end of the process, the interviewer can be smug in their initial assessment. 'See,' they may say, 'I told you that she was boring/intelligent/conscientious/arrogant. Here is all the evidence.' Yet this is selective evidence and the rest of it lies discarded.

This is important to consider at short-listing time as well as at interview because, even before meeting the candidate, this process is already taking place. 'As soon as I saw that she went to that college, I knew that she would be highly intelligent/condescending' or 'The fact that he is a keen golfer told me all I needed to know. The interview just confirmed all that.'

Short-listing

The recommendation is that all applications are scanned on arrival in case there are queries that need to be addressed immediately, and a holding letter sent thanking the applicant for their interest. This will often be done by the regional representative. Taking a half-baked and cursory look may not be a good tactic: you are likely to judge immediately with your heart rather than making a considered and fair assessment on the basis of a structured process. An initial decision is often made on the most irrelevant criteria: for example, whether someone uses paragraphs or bullet points in the form. This may have some importance in the selection criteria, but it is not the only or most critical priority!

Once the deadline for applications has passed, think about which stakeholders need to set aside time to sit down with all the applications and go through them together. There are two steps to this process:

1 matching against your needs from the person profile;
2 identifying additional 'added value' of the candidate.

Use a basic grid to record how each candidate measures up against your needs from the person profile. This will enable clear thinking based on evidence. Add a section that captures any added value of the candidate that you can see, such as calling, competence or chemistry, which may not have been part of your profile but would bring something extra to your church.

Some regions recommend short-listing with the name and other personal details removed so that there is no room for unintentional bias.

Remember that the candidate is likely to have had experience within ministry and other environments – in the workplace or as a volunteer. This evidence might be just as valuable to your context as their experience in ministry.

A minister applied for a job straight from their curacy. Their previous job had been as managing director of a care facility where they had managed clients with diverse needs who needed to access a variety of different services. A key skill for this person was to be aware of what they didn't know and to know where to find it out. Johari's window[2] identifies the difference between someone who knows that they have a gap in understanding (conscious incompetence) and someone who does not (unconscious incompetence). When a candidate has a gap, if they are consciously incompetent and have evidence of being in roles where they have had to find out and act on external advice, you are beginning to build a picture that the gap is a measured risk.

Measurement for short-listing and beyond

Matching what you see and hear against your needs is an analytical process. This is how we suggest you do it.

- *Step 1* Start with the statements from the person profile and identify which are essential and which are desirable. Essential attributes are not scored. Any applicants who do not have all the characteristics deemed essential will not be taken further.
- *Step 2* Look at the desirable attributes. These should be rated on a 1 to 10 scale, with 10 being most important. Only one attribute can be rated 10. Other statements may be rated at the same level of importance – in the example in Table 13.2, 'has had experience of developing fresh expressions' is weighted the same as 'has over-seen a large church-building project'. Once the relative weighting has been agreed, determine how each applicant's form will be measured against it. A simple method would be to use a 1 to 10 scale again, with 10 showing that the evidence provided totally fits the statement, 8 meaning the evidence mostly fits the statement and 5 meaning there is a little fit. The tool could be in a spreadsheet format, with formulas to enable the automatic calculation of the scores, or as a paper sheet attached to each application and compiled and calculated by hand. You can use this blank grid again in the interview and rescore as you uncover evidence. This process is best done in collaboration, to ensure that you have agreement as you go, rather than dealing with differences of opinion once you have completed scores.
- *Step 3* Identify any 'added value' information which can be gleaned from the application. Each statement needs to be given a rating on the same scale as Step 2. From all the candidates' added value, you will need to decide your rank of importance: is having a musical background more or less of a priority than taking school assemblies?

Finally, total all the scores. This gives you an indication of how this candidate fits based on the evidence they have provided against your

Table 13.2 **Example of a rating system**

	Step 1: Essential	Step 2: Desirable	Step 3: Added value
Is visible in the parish and the community	✓		
Will support, develop and inspire licensed and lay ministry	✓		
Is a great speaking communicator	✓		
Is passionate about developing prayer	✓		
Will lead school assemblies		3	
Is an experienced fund-raiser		6	
Is keen to develop fresh expressions		10	
Has had experience of successfully developing fresh expressions		7	
Has had experience of managing a team		8	
Is familiar with inner-city issues		9	
Has overseen a large-scale church-building project		7	

person profile. If their application indicates that they are a world-champion preacher, this will not be given a high score if it is not a priority from your audit, although it could be noted as added value. Remember that your scoring system does not judge them as a person, nor does it judge the quality of their spiritual life or anything other than how closely the evidence they provided meets the needs which you have identified.

If you have had enough applications, all the candidates you short-list should match the essential criteria from your person profile. If they do not, you need to think about re-advertising. So, from now on, you will also be appointing on

- calling to your church, now
- chemistry: style and fit with the rest of the team
- unique selling points.

Unique selling point

A friend was going to buy a new car and had decided on the decision-making criteria. It had to have a 1.4 engine, be economical on fuel and be red! Going around the car showrooms, it was clear that every red 1.4 Supermini fitted these criteria. They were essentially the same, but one car had something extra and our friend realized that this would provide many more possibilities. The back seats folded up and down to provide two different storage solutions. It had magic seats – and this meant that the car could carry bicycles, wheelchairs and large plants, which was very useful but outside the original criteria. The magic seats made the car the preferred buy. All your candidates will have magic seats or unique selling points which may not be part of your criteria-setting. Your job is to find them. Theirs is to share them.

In order to determine chemistry, refer back to the work you did in auditing your parish and understanding the current make-up of the team. As well as a broad understanding of personality types, this may include understanding the skills and skills gaps in the current team. Chemistry does not mean that you all have to be the same, but that you all need to work together so that, as a whole, you can be effective. An effective team is more likely to be a diverse team who recognize each other's differences and bring different approaches.

What else do we know already?

References

References do not tend to play a part in decision-making in the commercial world and often give no more information than confirmation of dates and job titles. If you receive a reference with this minimal information, do not assume that something is being hidden. It is more likely that the organization's policy is to provide only this detail. A personal reference may provide more, but the author may be biased towards the applicant's strengths. Organizations used to look with suspicion on a glowing reference from a manager: Why, one would ask, are they trying to rid themselves of this person?

In the Church, references are sometimes given more weight. They may provide some honest information about the candidate's capacity to meet the needs of the person profile – or they may not! If the applicant has chosen their referees well – and asked them to comment specifically on certain aspects of their experience – they may provide additional evidence which has not been described in the application form, as well as verifying data. Personal references and references from within the Church are more likely to provide useful data for your process, which can be added to other evidence to give a more complete picture. If you have queries about a reference, pick up the phone and ask for clarification from the referee: most people will be willing to help if asked.

Other information

Anecdotal information is not the most robust source of evidence but, added into the general mix, could be useful. Listening out for intelligence should be done carefully: an application is made in confidence and this should not be compromised by careless investigation. Similarly, the information which is gleaned from hearsay needs to be handled carefully: it may constitute little more than gossip or one person's personal opinion.

Meeting up

Talking to clergy about their experiences at interviews makes it clear how keen churches are to provide a thorough process . . . and candidates regularly pay a price for these good intentions. It's easy to get so caught up in the thought of meeting your potential new minister that you lose sight of the process and embark on a selection day(s) that is akin to a mad dash around the supermarket, picking at random things you like the look of. We have often heard of days where the candidates had almost no time to go to the toilet, let alone think, pray and reflect, as a result of an overfull programme. They are often desperate to work out a way of creating space in an interview day without upsetting you.

The meeting may include:

- a pre-event conversation or visit
- worship or prayer
- a familiarization tour
- meeting with a wider group of people
- audition
- interview.

The selection process

For each piece of the selection process, ensure that there is a broad and clear objective. The regional representative will have ideas of what should be included here, and you will need to work together to make this effective. If there is no purpose for an activity then do not do it. Worship and prayer are not part of the selection process: it is not a time for observations to be made which will be included in the decision-making! Table 13.3 gives some examples.

Some of this is more for the benefit of the candidate than the church, but the church benefits from allowing the minister time and

Table 13.3 The purpose of different aspects of the selection process

Activity	Purpose	Outcome for parish	Outcome for candidate
Familiarization tour	Candidates see church(es), house and community or location	A more informed candidate	Useful data which will help in candidate's decision-making process
Meetings with staff and clergy	Data-gathering for the candidate: how do things work around here?	A more informed candidate with an understanding of the chemistry	Useful data: may raise questions to bring to interview
Death by quiche	Candidates see the people: data-gathering for candidate	Parish feedback: nothing *or* questions for interview brought to the church reps	Useful data: may raise questions to bring to interview
Audition	To see candidate in action and gather observable data	Observation of ability in specific situation	Opportunity to demonstrate ability – what do you want them to know about you by the end of this?
Interview	To gather data about candidate's evidence of ability: calling, competence and chemistry	Evidence gathered in order to measure against job requirements	Evidence presented to meet job requirements; clarification questions asked of parish

space to build up a greater understanding of the role and the context. A more informed candidate means that the interview will be more valuable, with the candidate asking more critical and considered questions. Some candidates may deselect themselves on the basis of what they have seen. This is helpful: if a candidate discovers that what is seen is not what they expected, the valuable time of both sides can be saved by not continuing a process which would not be productive for anyone. Some churches separate the familiarization tour from the interview by as much as a week.

Familiarization tour

Familiarization will involve candidates having the opportunity to look around the plant and the place and to meet some of the people. If it is only familiarization you need to make this really clear to all those the candidates will encounter on the way. If not, again, clarity is the key.

The plant   This includes the church and its buildings as well as the house. Although it will be great for candidates to be shown what is where, they may equally value the additional opportunity to look round on their own and have time to reflect on whether they can see themselves living and working in this place. It's therefore worth having a guide who will loiter outside and allow them time to think.

The place   Go back to your audit of the church in the community and design a route which will allow the candidates to take in the culture and demographics of the place and get a real insight into the social and economic characteristics of the parish or community. Remember, this is not a tourist drive. For example, some may include an industrial or business area, and so the candidates should be driven past factories and warehouses as well as into social and private housing to see what the parish is really like.

This is a good opportunity to invite people from the congregation to be the drivers for each tour.

Give the candidates a map of the area. Clearly mark

- the parish boundaries, where relevant
- the location of the church(es)
- the location of churches of other denominations

- schools
- other public buildings
- public toilets.

Again, you will all benefit if the candidates have time to reflect, so it can be useful to drop them somewhere and also leave them time to explore on their own. If that's near a pub or a coffee shop, you are also giving them a place to sit if that's what they need.

Meetings with staff and clergy

This might be other leaders in your church or the paid staff team if there is one. It could also include leaders of other churches in your area. Again, briefing is the key. It needs to be clear to the candidate and the people whether this is simply an encounter and a conversation or whether it will form part of the interview process. Equally, some candidates have suddenly found themselves expected to ask formal questions to the people they encounter like this.

Death by quiche

In the Church of England, the parish representatives carry the responsibility of organizing the selection process and it is they who take part in the interviews. In the Methodist Church it will be the church and circuit stewards. As the church is much more than the representatives it is good to give candidates an opportunity to meet more people.

This is commonly known by clergy as 'death by quiche' or 'trial by wine', and can be an exhausting and overwhelming encounter which makes it difficult to have a level playing field. Introverts are expected to be social angels after a long and draining day in unfamiliar company. Extroverts find the experience energizing and exciting and may appear more appealing and sexy. Either way, the candidate can come away feeling as though they have been part of a game of wink murder when the winking was done behind their back – or, worse still, that they have been on the wrong end of a firing squad with people launching random questions. Equally, if you make the purpose and the rules of engagement clear to all the guests, it can become a productive and creative encounter where the church council or others feel engaged and the candidates get a much wider sense of some of the community which comprises your church congregation. Keep this in mind as you plan, considering the logistics and dynamics so that candidates come away feeling clearer about the chemistry to add to their discernment process.

Audition

A good indication of how a candidate will perform in practice is to see them perform as part of the selection process. After all, part of ministry is about public presence. The decision about subject matter must come out of your selection process. What do you expect to know about the candidate after the audition which you did not know beforehand? Is it that you want to have a sense of comfort that the candidate can indeed stand up and talk? Is it that you want to be bowled over by their passion and zeal?

Church and regional representatives need to consider how this can be usefully delivered to give more data. Should it be

- a ten-minute exposition of an agreed text in the form of a sermon?
- a talk and activity developed for all-age worship?
- a presentation about how the church might engage more effectively in the community?
- a facilitated activity?

Remember to be clear with the candidates well in advance about what the audition is for. Are they talking to you, the panel, or are they addressing you as a particular stakeholder group in the community: the congregation, the school assembly or the community hall? We have seen some good candidates not performing well at audition as they were uncertain or unconvinced about who they believed their audience was. Clunky announcements through the presentation, 'For this bit, if you could pretend to be five years old . . .' are awkward and can be avoided by clear communication from you about the parameters and expectations of the audition.

Whatever you decide, you will need to agree criteria and measurement with the selection panel so that you are all agreed on what you are looking for and so that there is a level playing field for all candidates. If this is not planned in advance, a less relevant and trivial factor may seem important: that the candidate appears nervous may be a fair observation but should not be the one criteria on which they are deselected. Considering criteria from the person profile is likely to be difficult and will need some hard thinking. We have been present when the selection panel has started engaging with the question of measurement, realized it was quite hard and so ended up deciding: 'Well, we'll just know whether they're right.' This lazy thinking is not fair for the candidate, as well as not being fair for the integrity of the process.

There will need to be space between one candidate's audition and their interview, because these require a different voice and different energy. The audition is a performance of a kind, and the interview is a conversation which may be quite personal. To expect the candidate to move from one to the other without a break is unrealistic: they need time to regroup, and without that you will not be giving them the maximum opportunity to demonstrate who they are.

Interview

However much this is meant to be discernment and selection on both sides, it can easily become a one-sided process where the power base rests firmly with the interviewing panel. The interview is designed to find out whether the candidate is right for you, but also whether they feel the church is right for them. So the ideal process is not one-sided but a two-way conversation in which both parties join in the discernment process together before the church makes a final decision. This is the approach that we advocate here: bringing forward the point at which the individual becomes fully involved as a participant in the process rather than becoming passive and submissive to whatever the selectors foist upon them. Here are some technical ideas about what you need in an effective interview to enable dialogue, discernment and selection.

Interview script

A script may feel artificial and an equal opportunities obligation, but it does not have to mean that only ten dry questions are asked. You need to be asking appropriate questions so that the candidate is given the opportunity to provide evidence. An interview script or standard opening questions which you develop for your context at this time are important, so that

- there is consistency for candidates: without an interview script, one candidate may be asked questions which allow them more opportunity to demonstrate their relevant experience;
- the questions meet the person profile;

- questions are asked only when they will be useful for the process;
- the candidate is clear what your questions mean;
- you are clear what your questions mean;
- you have a way of comparing different candidates against the person profile.

As you create your interview script, think about why you want to ask these questions. What sort of answer are you expecting? Will this question give you the evidence you need to keep candidates in or take them out of the decision-making process? If not, then don't ask it.

Some stakeholders will have a standard script that they always use at interviews. Some negotiation may be required so that the interview script meets your particular person profile and their needs.

Themes

Take the themes from the person profile. You will be looking for evidence to measure

- whether a candidate can do something (competence);
- how they do it (chemistry).

The candidates you see will have been through selection and training, so you can assume that they meet general standards of competence. If you are concerned that you may have missed something out, here is an example of the Church of England selection criteria:

- vocation (calling)
- ministry within the Church (calling)
- spirituality (calling)
- personality and character (chemistry)
- relationships (chemistry)
- leadership and collaboration (competence and chemistry)
- faith (calling and competence)
- mission and evangelism (calling and competence)
- quality of mind (competence).

These criteria may be useful hooks on which to hang your themes from the person profile.

Once the interview script is complete, check back to make sure that you have questions that will provide evidence for all the themes, and that there are no questions which are not directly hung on them.

Types of questions

A good question is incisive, is easy to understand and will elicit the evidence you require. If the person profile requires someone who has created a strategy for their church, you could ask about their ability to do this in a number of ways:

- 'How would you create a strategy for your church?' may provide evidence of an individual's ability to be creative under pressure and dream up an approach on the spot. This is useful if the profile states that there is a need to be spontaneously strategic under pressure, but may not give you the information you require if you want evidence of robust and effective strategy. This is a hypothetical question, and at best all you will receive from it is hypothetical evidence.
- 'Do you feel that it is important for a church to have a strategy?' You may want to discover how high a priority strategy is for this individual, but this is a leading question. Only the most moronic individual would answer 'no' to this.
- 'Have you ever written a strategy?' may just give you a 'yes' or a 'no' and would need a further question to get a valuable response. Closed questions are good to slow down a verbose talker, but overuse of these at interview will not help to gather the requisite evidence. Overuse of closed questions turns a conversation into an oral questionnaire.
- Multiple questions tend to be asked when questions have not been prepared: 'I'd like to ask you about your church strategy. Is there one? Are you the person who devised it or who did you devise it with? I'm presuming it must have been a corporate decision, or at least some it must have been. So what steps did you take, or would you recommend, if you were giving advice to another church? Is there anything particular?' This question tells the candidate more about the interviewer's state of mind and lack of planning than about what it is that the interviewer needs to learn about the candidate. A clued-up candidate may respond: 'Which question would you like me to answer?' to clarify matters and make sure that the focus of the answer is appropriate to the need.

Evidence-based questions

Although, for interest's sake, you might be inclined to ask the question, 'How would you cope if the coffee rota ladies went on strike?'

Table 13.4 Framework for evidence-based questions

Describe	What did you do?
	What happened as a result?
	What did it involve?
Illustrate	How did it come about?
	What was the reason for it?
Appraise	Why do you think that was?
	How important was that?
Personal opinion	What did you think about it?
Considered judgement	What were the advantages of doing it that way?
	How effective was it?
	How could the problem have been avoided?
Reaction	How did you react to that?
	So, what did you do?
Feelings	What did you feel about it?

you may as well be asking the question, 'How would you handle the four horsemen of the apocalypse?' Hypothetical questions are not evidence-based. They do not establish what has happened in the past, and therefore do not predict the future.

The most effective question is the one which elicits an example. 'Give me an example of a strategy you have created and implemented successfully' will give you factual evidence. With a real example to focus on, follow-up questions should be easy. A flow as shown in Table 13.4 means that a great deal of evidence can be drawn from one example. Some of these questions may be answered as the candidate speaks, and this is a useful checklist if you need to ask follow-up questions to ensure that you have the evidence you need.

Evidence-based questions are based in reality, which means that you get a truer picture of what the candidates have done.

Questions not to ask

Best practice states that there are questions that should not be asked at interview to ensure that no discrimination occurs. Sometimes interviewers feel that this diminishes their ability to select the appropriate candidate: Alan Sugar stated that if he is unable to ask whether a woman is intending to have children, then he is less likely to employ a woman. But employers who feel that the detail of legislation is 'political correctness gone mad' miss its value in protecting individuals and society.

In short, it is not acceptable for a decision-making question to be discriminatory.

Some factors may need to be taken into account to enable the individual to perform their work. For example, it is useful to know that the house would need a wheelchair ramp: but the question is not about selection, rather about practical application. A question such as 'Is there anything that we need to be aware of or to do in order for you to work effectively?' will give the candidate the opportunity to share this information with you. It is a practical logistical question, not a decision-making one.

Some weird and wonderful questions are asked at interviews, which makes one wonder what sort of evidence is being collected. 'What is your favourite TV programme?' 'If you were an animal, what sort of animal would you be?' 'What's your favourite colour?' 'What is the last book you read?' – any of these may be of interest to you, just for curiosity's sake, but what will you do with the answer? Does one answer indicate that a candidate is within your criteria and another outside? Rather than giving clear evidence, such answers give information which may be interpreted and become false evidence. If the last book I read was embarrassing chick-lit nonsense, I may instead tell you of a serious theological tome. If you then interpret on my behalf that I am a solemn and humourless individual, we have together been complicit in moving away from fact-based evidence into sweeping and broad assumptions. Questions like this add little or nothing to the interview process. You cannot second-guess candidates on the basis of their responses. If you like these questions, they are better used at a blind date than an interview.

Questions that seem standard, such as 'What are your strengths and weaknesses?' should only be asked if they provide evidence for one of your themes. It is difficult to think what theme this would apply to. Even if 'self-awareness' was a theme, this question would still be limited in what evidence it could provide. As you may know very little about the candidate, it would be difficult to measure how accurate the response to this question might be and therefore how self-aware they were.

In addition to questions based on the person profile, there may be a few 'complete package' questions that you would like to ask:

- If we get you, what do we get?
- Why do you want to be *our* minister?

- What's the biggest mistake you made in your last parish and what did you do about it?

These can be useful in listening out for calling to this job and for chemistry with your team.

Planning the interviews

Consider how the interview will play out. Will the interview be done to or done with the candidate? Eighteen people in a room firing questions at a candidate is not an effective way of getting the best out of someone. It cannot be a dialogue and is more like *Question Time* without the measured moderation of David Dimbleby. Are you looking for a minister for your church or someone who can withstand a grilling by 18 people? The fewer interviewers present, the better, and these should include church representatives and regional representatives. As we are recommending that discussions and decisions happen post-interview (after evidence-gathering) it may be that all the decision-makers do not need to be present at the interview, as long as all the evidence is collated in an effective manner so that those not present are able to review it.

Some parishes organize a series of interviews, but we hear that this can sometimes be badly planned, with all interviews consisting of similar questions. That means some questions do not get asked at all. If you decide to have more than one interview, ensure that the interview scripts are written in partnership so that there is no duplication of questions.

Clear communication

As you have worked on ensuring that each activity has purpose, it is important to communicate this to all those involved. Everyone needs to be clear about what is familiarization and what is selection. One minister went to what they thought was a familiarization day and was put in front of a panel of parishioners for a formal interview. Another minister was concerned that no one at 'death by quiche' was asking her any questions and assumed that this was because they were not interested in her as a candidate: in fact, the church council had been well briefed that this was the candidate's opportunity to find out about the church so were doing as they were told. The candidate, unfortunately, did not know this.

Table 13.5 A briefing document

Activity	Familiarization?	Discernment?	Selection?
Familiarization tour	Candidate	Candidate	
Death by quiche	Candidate	Candidate	
Meetings with staff and clergy	Church and candidate	(Church and candidate)*	(Church and candidate)*
Audition		Church	Church
Interview	Church	Church	Church

* If the meetings with staff and clergy are part of the discernment and selection process the candidate needs to know this, and there should be objective measures for this activity too.

A briefing document (see Table 13.5) which is the same for everyone demonstrates transparency and makes explicit what each activity is for.

Interview preparation for candidates

Consider the interview as your opportunity to demonstrate evidence for what you have done, how you did it and what you might do in this place in the future. That is as grand or as fearsome as it gets. If this is what the interview is for, then to prepare well you need to prepare examples or evidence. You are more likely to be successful in an exam by revising and practising rather than being surprised by the questions that are asked: it is the same at interview. As in an exam, you need to be ready with your data rather than a preconceived answer or script, as you do not know what you will be asked. Good preparation means that interviewers meet the real you.

Practical evidence will be more valuable than theoretical. If interviewers ask a question about managing conflict, a theoretical answer may be, 'I would listen carefully to each party and then try to facilitate a conversation between them in a way which would make them both feel safe.' This does not demonstrate that you have managed conflict! On the other hand, 'During that difficult situation, I listened carefully to each party and tried to facilitate a conversation between them. I did that with two home group leaders and it was very effective: the outcome was . . .' makes for a more effective evidence-based answer which places theory in a real situation. A robust answer should include evidence, the action taken and what happened as a result.

You will have pulled out themes from the person profile and any other research that you have done around the church context. You may feel confident enough to speak with the church representatives about the themes on which they will be looking for evidence prior to the selection day, in order to concentrate on those most relevant to them.

Once you have established what is important to the church, the next step is to identify examples which demonstrate your ability in this area. Be practical as well as reflective. Writing lists or drawing mind maps will enable you to visually recall your evidence. Or write down key words which will remind you of the example and evidence, e.g. 'Doris'. You could plot evidence in a table such as Table 13.6 overleaf. There may be other methods you can think of which will act as an aide memoire.

The process by which you will be delivering the required evidence is shown in Figure 13.1.

You may have identified a theme title which uses different language from the interviewer's. Pause and consider where *their* question fits into *your* structure of identified themes. A practical example of this is shown in Figure 13.2.

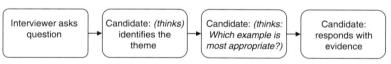

Figure 13.1 **Delivering evidence**

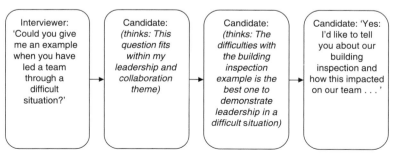

Figure 13.2 **Fitting your theme to the interviewer's question**

Table 13.6 An example of a table of evidence

Theme	Example	Activity	Results
Leading prayer	Building labyrinth for Holy Week	As activity for local schools and others in Holy Week; used talents of congregation and others in working group	Four local primary schools sent KS2 classes: that means we saw about 720 children, as well as others from local community. Useful outreach which has meant a number of new faces in church
	Prayer retreat	Led prayer retreat for 40 of our congregation: mixed group. Driven from need identified by members of the congregation	Successful retreat: use of silence and discipline of prayer proved to be very moving. Two weekly prayer groups set up by participants independently
Inter-faith collaboration	Set up and ran Inter-faith collaboration group as curate in previous church	Many faith groups in the town: the group met quarterly with representatives from five non-Christian organizations and three Christian organizations	Many good outcomes including sharing of resources and buildings, joint support for community initiatives, increased understanding
	Agreements made that weekly Muslim mothers' group meets in church hall	Mothers' group needed a meeting place; needed to work to encourage some key members of the congregation to support this	Group has been meeting for 18 months now and feels welcome. Greater understanding
	Speaker at inter-faith network	Asked to speak about barriers and solutions in building local collaborations	Talk went well with some interest from local newspapers

Listening carefully to the question, make sure that you understand fully what evidence is required, and if necessary clarify to check that you are connecting the question correctly with the theme:

Here is my example → This is what I did → This is what happened.

Not all the evidence you provide needs to close with a happy ending. Some might include unresolved issues or unsatisfactory outcomes. Be realistic about situations that are still being handled or issues that you have dealt with in the past which you may choose to handle differently now. That is still good evidence.

As well as being clear on the skills you have demonstrated from the church, remember to include skills which you have used successfully in other settings. Your experience as a team leader may have come not from ministry but from a previous role in industry. Recognizing transferable skills that you have when you have not got the exact experience required is valuable prior to attending the interview. Many leaders become ministers later in life and so have a wealth of experience to bring from other contexts. In the heightened pressure of the interview seat, it is impossible to start considering these for the first time.

If you are struggling with the concept of evidence, step out of your own shoes for a moment. Think about people who know you and what their perception of you may be. What would Mrs Smith who sits in the back row have to say about you? What about the young people? How would the churchwarden describe you? It may be that looking at yourself through others' eyes can help you capture more evidence.

Once you have created your mind map or table which details the themes and evidence, then practise! Try taking the framework for evidence-based questions in Table 13.4 and ask yourself these questions for each of your examples. Involving someone else with this would be even more useful. It will help you to become fluent in talking about yourself and providing effective responses which will meet the needs of the interviewer. You are not learning rote answers, simply familiarizing yourself with your evidence.

There will undoubtedly be questions asked in the interview which are not addressed by your neat evidence and example table. One benefit of this approach to preparation is that the majority of questions should create no surprise and you will be able to go into the interview with a sense of calm and control rather than panic. Like success in exams, successful interviews are based on effective preparation. All we want is that the interviewers meet you.

As well as preparing your evidence, there will be a point in the interview where you are asked whether you have any questions. Prepare for this, too. An absence of questions – or indeed, an awkward silence while the candidate racks her brain, mangled already by the interview process, to think of any remotely intelligent question – is a painful way to end an interview. Note down some questions about the church, the community, activities or more general subjects so that no thinking needs to be done on the hoof.

Decision-making

The decision-making needs to be free from discrimination: we have talked about this in relation to interview questions, and maintaining integrity through the decision-making process is vital. There will inevitably be some bias which is based on previous experiences and which should be recognized as such. Maybe there has been some bad experience in the past with a male colleague. Because of this past experience, it is unhelpful to generalize that the issue lay in gender, but a realization that this individual was not the right fit in that team is more positive. The fact that he is male, has brown hair and a faint West Country accent, or that his middle name is Martin is not the reason that things didn't work out. Those aspects of someone you have come across in the past should not be brought into the current decision-making frame to confuse the issue. Concentrating on what you do know about the candidates and the evidence they bring is what is important.

This example demonstrates how easily we can make false assumptions based on previous experience; the other insidious form of discrimination is intolerances founded on personal bias. Everyone is accountable in the decision-making process, and if you believe that there is covert discrimination in your selection process it is your responsibility to voice this concern clearly.

UK employers are subject to the Equality Act which protects people from discrimination including on grounds of race, gender and age. Changes in legislation and case law mean that guidance provided here would be quickly out of date, therefore you need to check the current situation and whether employment legislation needs to be taken into account as part of your selection process. Good practice suggests that the spirit of the legislation is useful: if you want to select the candidate who is called, competent and with the right chemistry, then other factors should be considered unimportant.

When organizations have turned down candidates on the basis that they may want to have a baby, they may have turned down the right candidate for the job. By deselecting on the basis of factors other than skills – for example age or gender – the pool of appropriate candidates becomes smaller. Your focus needs to be on the right person for your job: if you or your church are intolerant of people from a particular ethnic group or a particular sexual orientation then this is something that will need to be dealt with. But the decision-making process is neither the time nor the place to do it. Your national church will have guidelines. For example, it is only acceptable to refuse to short-list women if your local church has a formal and agreed policy to do this: in the Church of England this is about agreeing Resolution A and B. The Methodist Conference reaffirms the traditional teaching of the Church on human sexuality, namely chastity for all outside marriage and fidelity within it.

But above any legal, moral or economic rationale, it is clear both from the Bible and from our own present-day experience that God calls all people regardless of their 'type'. It is therefore completely unacceptable to make a decision that in your church you need a particular gender, ethnic group or age, or to decide that owing to a disability a candidate should not be selected. We are informed that human distinctions that are made on the grounds of race or gender are not of God and therefore we have no right to bring this into the selection process.[3]

As well as planning to make decisions based on evidence and not bias, consider the questions that you will be asking and on which you will base your decisions. Do they fit? Do they find out what you need to know about calling, competence and chemistry? What do candidates bring that we had not thought of? Focusing your mind during planning on how you will make decisions will develop a useful thread that will run right through discernment and selection.

As you plan for decision-making, it is advisable to have a frank and honest conversation with the regional representative to determine whether the process is really open and transparent. It may be that you and the candidates all go through the process in good faith, yet at the final step your preferred candidate through discernment and selection is turned down in favour of another. To avoid this disappointment, establish from the outset under what circumstances any external information might be brought in. If all the candidates appear to be similar in one area, might the regional representative then bring forward their knowledge of the aptitude or otherwise of one of the candidates? If so, is this a level playing field? The regional representative may only know of the ministers who are in their region, which possibly puts the others at an unfair advantage – or disadvantage! The candidate who has come from a different region has no advocate in the room: this should be recognized earlier than at the decision-making meeting.

> We pray together as fellow travellers:
> Help us see what can be achieved together in Your name.
> Be with us in our discernment.
> Lead us in our decision-making.

14

The process in action

In this chapter we will investigate how the selection process works in action. Your preparation has been done. Now it's time to roll your sleeves up and get on with the job in hand.

Applications

Once the advert has been posted, your profile is listed in the stationing handbook or the search committee are fully in action, you may sit back and wait for a flood of applications to descend. Often the regional representative will receive the applications. For one-at-a-time appointments this may not involve so much paperwork, but there is still a process to undertake.

There is a thrill to seeing your vacancy go live, and thinking about potential applicants who may be reading it over their breakfast cereal or their laptop and be excited by the prospect of working in your church. Be prayerful: ask God to open people's eyes and guide those who might be right for your church(es). If no one comes forward, go back to the profile and advert and ask a third party to give you some feedback.

The church representatives have worked hard to get to this point. Now it is time to wait for that to bear fruit. This is the time for potential applicants to get busy: to request parish profiles, person specs and application forms; to spend time listening for God's guidance; to find out whether they can fit their family into the house; to consider the practicalities of a move to your area of the country. This could be quite an anxious time for the applicant, when conversations need to happen with their family and decisions about what the future may hold become more real. Once they have decided to apply, the applicant will want to give you evidence that they might meet your essential criteria, providing you with the evidence that will mean you short-list them without question and they join you in a mutual discernment process.

Pre-interview process

John Lee, the Church of England Clergy Appointments Adviser, says that to work effectively the appointments process needs to be a conversation, otherwise it risks becoming play-acting on one or both sides. Would you make an offer on a house without looking round it? That's what you are asking candidates to do if there is no pre-interview process at all.

To produce a quality application, candidates may want to find out more about the job or the place. In our experience churches don't know what to do with that, and some regional representatives actively discourage it. Stand in the candidate's shoes. They are considering moving their home, their job, their family and their place of worship all at once. If this is to be a discernment process they need space and opportunity to see the place. Some may choose to attend a service or coffee mornings – or they might send a spy. More confident applicants may wish to speak with you or meet with you, asking questions about the place. This is to be encouraged and managed well.

In the Church, there seems to be some general apathy by applicants to gather information – as if it might be considered cheating in some way. Do you want your next minister to be someone who is interested enough in your context to ask some questions about it? However challenging that might be?

Think about:

- How will you deal with questions from potential applicants – will they go through to a particular individual to answer?
- Would you be prepared to put aside some time to meet a potential applicant to describe the parish and its potential in more detail?

A good applicant may be put off by a blunt rejection of a request for some more information: this may be interpreted as evidence of how unfriendly and impersonal the church is. Including a note to applicants in your communication pack, informing them where to address their questions, creates a more level playing field: then all have the opportunity to make contact if they wish. Otherwise you will find that only the one applicant who has the confidence to pick up the phone will do so, getting all their questions answered and thus having an advantage.

Reality hits

Once you have received the applications, your process goes live. There might be a surprise: clergy are diverse and this is likely to be reflected in the applications that come in. Through this process you have been focusing on what the parish is like and who you need to lead you into the next season. We have asked you to lay aside the detail about the future minister: subconsciously, your expectation may be that they will be the same as (or very different from) the previous minister. Instead, you have applicants who include a 40-something female with a large family, people who are divorced or not married, or someone who has not been ordained for long, has no children or is 59.

This may challenge some preconceptions, purely because it was not what you were expecting. Most of it will make little difference on how the individual performs in the job: there are, however, some exceptions.

What you discover here should not impact whether you short-list the individual, but you may consider what else you need to know about someone to make the right decision. One of your applicants may not have been ordained long and there may be some gaps in their level of knowledge as a result. If the individual has not, for example, been in a post where they have had to deal with applying for a faculty, check whether a more experienced mentor in another church is sufficient to be able to support them.

Assumptions can be made by deriving insight erroneously from the information provided. A parish priest who has one more job in her before retirement may not have the level of enthusiasm of the 45-year-old who has given up previous career and aspirations to follow his vocation – but equally she may do! As you go through the applications, keep notes of what additional information is required for you to gain a complete picture of the individual, to make the work required for the interview easier.

Added value

Going through applications, you may find that an applicant has some fantastic experience that had not been considered when you put together your person profile. There may be other valuable assets that an applicant has which may change your perception of what you really need. What are the applicants' unique selling points? Or magic seats?

Ensuring that all your short-listed applicants meet the essential criteria means that you can measure again on the basis of added value. Consider what this unique selling point might bring to the church and to the community. Is this something that they would be excited to develop further?

Make sure that you still use your short-listing criteria and do not discard them in your enthusiasm about added value.

Communication to candidates

Candidates should be contacted as soon as short-listing decisions have been made; regional representatives may be responsible for this. They need information about the selection process, including what will be involved. If there is to be an audition as part of the process, candidates should be informed of the context, subject, time parameters and any other useful information. Providing candidates with a named point of contact will be valuable for them to ask questions about the event itself. It's not unusual for candidates to receive this information at the last minute. That does not serve anyone.

Selection day or days

You will want the selection days to run smoothly, and so focusing on the logistical detail is important. Some tips you may want to consider:

- Keep the candidates apart as much as possible.
- Give them space and time to think and pray.
- Give yourselves time to think and pray: ensure that the church is praying in parallel with the activities of the day.
- Ask in advance if they have school-aged children and would like to visit a school before the formal part of the process – or a care home, if that is what's appropriate for the individual.
- Walk through the day in your mind before it happens. Consider the impact that every part of the plan will have on the candidates.
- Think about who to invite: do candidates come with their partners? If the candidate has family, you would love to meet them all . . . but this is a selection process for the minister and different people wish

to have a different level of involvement. Partners may be unable to take time off work. They may have small children, and it could be very disruptive for the candidate to be worrying both about the interview and about the family. Remember, none of this context should be used as evidence in the discernment process. Family invitations can imply bias against single candidates.

- You may want to consider allowing candidates to come and look round the church, community and house before the interview day.
- Your congregation will want to know everything about the candidates. Remember that the candidates may not have told their own churches that they are looking for a move, so be sensitive about how much information you divulge.
- Badges will facilitate introductions. The candidate's badge only needs to say their first name.
- Remember to ask whether the candidates or their companions have any special dietary requirements.

On the subject of food, think about what you need to offer throughout the day and whether the food breaks are downtime or another part of the process. If they are downtime, leave the candidates space to eat. If you are planning a social over food or drink, make sure that what is provided is easy to chew, preferably not tomato-colour and easily mobile. Think along the spectrum, with Spaghetti Bolognese being the least friendly dish to serve. Believe it or not, one candidate had to eat pork chops in a social setting while people were asking interview-style questions.

Timetable

The timetable for the day may look something like Table 14.1 overleaf, depending on the activities that will be undertaken in your particular selection process. Designing the timetable in this way ensures that everyone involved (this might be drivers as well as clergy and staff) understands what is required from them and when.

Following this process for the candidates, the final discernment and selection process for the panel will also need to be scheduled.

Death by quiche

Your parish guests need to be clear, before they arrive, about what happens after the social meeting. This is not *The X Factor*, where the

Table 14.1 Selection day timetable

	Candidate 1	*Candidate 2*	*Candidate 3*
10–10.30	Welcome and prayers in the church	Welcome and prayers in the church	Welcome and prayers in the church
10.30	Meeting with staff, meeting with group clergy Break	Look at Church A	Look round the vicarage
11.30	Look round the vicarage	Break Meeting with staff, meeting with group clergy	Look at Church A
12.30	Space to think in village pub	Space to think in village pub	Space to think in village pub
1.30	Look at Church A	Look at Church B	Drive around parish
2.30	Drive around parish	Look round the vicarage	Look at Church B
3.30	Look at Church B	Drive around parish	Break Meeting with staff, meeting with group clergy
4.30	Formal day activities close	Formal day activities close	Formal day activities close
6.00	Meal with church council	Meal with church council	Meal with church council
7.30	Compline or Evening Prayer Overnight in hotel	Compline or Evening Prayer Overnight in hotel	Compline or Evening Prayer Overnight in hotel
9.00	Morning prayers	Morning prayers	Morning prayers
9.30	Interview		
10.30	Audition		
11.30	End of process	Interview	
12.30	(Lunch)	Audition	(Lunch)
1.30		End of process	Interview
2.30		(Lunch)	Audition
3.30			End of process

guests score the candidates as they leave the room, having seen and experienced only a small part of who they are in an artificial situation. There are times, however, when someone may have picked up a clue which raises an important question for the interview. If you have decided that guests at this meeting will feed into the interview process, you will need to ensure their questions are captured. Some of these will have already been answered in the paperwork or references to which only you have access. And sometimes it will be a key question which you will need to include in the interview. If their question is derived from an incident or comment that took place during the evening, be careful to check whether it is a fair and reasonable question to ask.

Interviewers' meeting

This may happen at the end of Day 1 or at the start of Day 2 and should consist of the church representatives and those involved in the discernment and selection processes. Ensure that all the data that has been gathered is collated and analysed. Is there anything that has been identified during the course of the day which needs follow-up in the interview? Is there a question that needs to be asked as a result? Download all this data and determine in collaboration what, if anything, needs to be done.

A layout like Table 14.2 may be useful to collect information from those who were with the candidates during the day. Remember to include what is in the application form.

At this point all the key stakeholders in the discernment and selection are present, so this meeting is critical for the process. There may be at least three separate groups on the panel: the regional representatives, the church representatives and patron or trustees. You want

Table 14.2 Collating information about the candidates

	Tour guide	Church council questions	Questions from clergy and staff
Information: Is there anything of interest that could or should be followed up at interview? **Outcomes:** Do we need to follow up? How?			

to be aligned as a panel rather than come across as three separate interviews in one room, so spending time determining how the interview and panel will operate is important. If the role of chair is not a given, you will need to assign it now. We know that sometimes this doesn't happen, and as result it is obvious to the candidate that the panel is not aligned and the experience is rather muddled. Respect for the candidate suggests that flying in at the last minute to do the interview may not be fair.

Last minute for candidates

Just as the interviewers will be meeting together to check their thinking and ensure that all is covered, the candidate ought to be going through a similar process.

- What have I learnt today that I did not know previously?
- What do I need to know more about?
- Is there something that seems important to the church that I have not prepared as evidence for interview – therefore, do I need to rethink any of the evidence that I have prepared?
- What do they need to know about me by the end of this process that they don't know now?

A critical question to ask at this point also is: am I still interested in the job? If the answer to this is no, it is worth analysing why this may be. As much as an interviewer can be put off by one negative trait that has been observed, the candidate also may have a niggling concern about one aspect of the church which taints their overall impression. Identifying what the concern is, and whether or not this is a deal-breaker, is useful before going into interview. Uncertainty and a lack of conviction can be visible, so determining how you feel about the role ahead of time would be useful.

Interview

In the interview, both parties will be trying to ensure that the required evidence is provided so that the church can answer the question: 'Is this candidate called, competent and with the right chemistry?' and the candidate can answer the question: 'Am I called, competent and is the chemistry right?'

All the representatives have planned the questions. The candidate has prepared their evidence. Now it is up to both sides to ensure that the required evidence is shared and that there is dialogue. Contrary to some schools of thought, making candidates feel uncomfortable and under pressure does not get the best out of them. Unless you are doing an experiential selection activity in order to demonstrate the individual's ability under pressure within an interview – which seems like an unlikely activity to be part of their job and therefore not an exercise to be encouraged – helping the individual feel comfortable so that they can share their evidence with you effectively is likely to be the best approach. Therefore, ensuring that they are comfortable, have had a toilet break and have a glass of water will all be useful and encouraging ways to behave. Smiling, warm handshakes and appropriate gentle humour can also be used effectively.

As the church representatives, your responsibility is to look after the candidate. You may feel that your priority is the visiting representatives, but attending to the needs of the candidates is important for all of you so that you can get the best out of them. Be aware that some candidates will need more warming up than others: in order to dissipate nerves, be prepared to engage in small talk. Let them tell you about their journey or how they slept that night. Letting them say something inconsequential helps them to get over the initial trauma of talking.

The interviewer

Once everyone has settled and is ready to begin, provide a warm introduction to the interview. Include:

- an introduction of all the panel members, including those who have been introduced beforehand (the candidate does not need added pressure about trying to remember names);
- a description of how the process will work. How long will the interview be? Are there sections in your interviews that the candidate can be made aware of? Do you want real examples of how the candidate has demonstrated their talents? Who will be asking the questions?
- an opportunity for the candidate to ask any questions on the process before the interview starts.

Keep the mood light and allow space for the candidate to think. Some candidates will need time to reflect on your question and come up with appropriate examples. It is more useful for you to have well-considered evidence from the candidate than a hasty answer to your question.

Make sure that you are giving the candidate full attention. Most people have at least one example of a 'bad' interview that they have been put through, and the reason that it is considered bad is often because of lack of attention. That might mean not being listened to fully, or not being allowed the agreed length of time in interview, or being distracted by something else (a mobile phone ringing being one example!). Even if they are really boring, make sure that you are fully present and there with the candidate: nodding, smiling, keeping eye contact are all signs that you are listening attentively. Do not scare the candidate with this behaviour to an extreme: eye contact which bores into the soul rather than gently supporting the individual will put them off.

Ensure that you are playing the role of interviewer for the whole interview. You may have accompanied the candidate on the familiarization trip, or chatted with them at lunch, or indeed may already know them. Make sure that you clearly wear the hat of the interviewer, which will allow the candidate to play their part appropriately as the interviewee.

Keeping the conversation on track

As your purpose is to receive evidence, you may need to support and direct the candidates to allow them to do their best. Sometimes candidates will reinterpret your questions and you may need to gently bring them back to the question you asked to ensure that you get the evidence you require. Candidates may believe that when you ask the question 'Give me an example . . .' they are being helpful in answering it in a generic way: 'What I would do is . . .' It will be a more effective process if you can bring them back to the specific, as you require evidence of actual fact rather than generalizations.

Sometimes candidates will refer to examples of activities by using 'we'. It may be that this is because the task was a joint one – or it may be that this is out of a sense of humility so that it is clear that responsibility for making the initiative happen was shared. It is useful to clarify this. If it is important that you discover what the candidate can do independently, ask, 'Which part of this was your responsibility?' If you find out that in actual fact this was a corporate piece of work, ask for another example: 'Would you be able to provide an example where you had overall responsibility for a project?'

We can recall interviews where the individual has provided the same example as a response to a number of different questions – and yes, it may be that one project did include teamwork, communication skills and negotiating. From the candidate's point of view it may feel as though this example is so important that it should be given as a response to as many answers as possible, but it will give a fairly limited picture of their experience. To give them the greatest opportunity to provide depth of evidence, it would be fair to indicate that a different example would be valuable.

The appropriate response to a candidate's answer is 'Thank you.' You are thanking them for providing the evidence that is required, and you are also closing that question.

Being clear and signposting what is happening – 'This next question is about worship . . .' – is useful for the nervous candidate, so it is good practice to let them know when you have received what you are after. However, do not offer false hope: 'Oooh, that *is* a good answer. Yes, excellent!' may give the candidate too great an expectation of how their response has landed.

The interview will speed by, so each moment counts. Ensure your questions are short and to the point, otherwise half of the interview time will be spent with the interviewer talking. If you feel that the candidate is going into too much detail or has not understood the question fully, do not let them continue burbling aimlessly but stop them, gently, either suggesting that you have enough evidence and are ready to move on or asking the question again. Another time-waster that interviewers are sometimes guilty of is becoming over-interested in the content of the answers. 'Cornwall, you say? Yes, a lovely part of the world and one in which Mavis and I have spent many happy holidays': with the interviewer's hat on you must ensure that you are evidence-collecting rather than joining in for a chat. And don't forget the dialogue!

It is difficult when the interviewer starts to feel involved pastorally. A candidate may wish to bring up a difficult experience from their past to illustrate a question: the interviewer needs to be able to notice this without becoming involved in it. If there is a strong sense that this candidate may require some further support, the interviewer may choose to talk to them privately after the interview rather than changing the parameters of the discussion.

Allow sufficient time for the candidate to ask questions that they may have. These may have been gathered during the process, or may be questions that they have not had the opportunity to ask. Rather than this being merely a politeness on your part, making sure that the candidate has the information that they require in order to make a decision is really important for the process. This is in addition to having a dialogue.

In the candidate's chair

The preparation the candidate does beforehand is critical. When the interview starts, consider whether there's anything further you need to be comfortable. If you are a reflective thinker, ask the interview panel if it's all right for you to pause in order to marshal your thoughts so that you can give them the evidence that they require. It is very likely that you will be nervous before and during the interview. You may feel out of control (although your preparation will definitely minimize this) and that the whole of the rest of your life is balancing on your success at this very moment: remember, it is quite normal to feel nervous. Rather than trying to pretend to yourself that you are highly confident, instead recognize the nerves and, having done that, focus your mind on the evidence you have prepared.

Keep in mind that the process is not one in which you are required to 'sell' yourself as if you were a vacuum cleaner salesperson. You do not need to be dishonest; you do not need to exaggerate excessively. Spin does not help. Your role in the interview is to give the interviewers the evidence they require. These are facts that they are after, and any sense of false humility is not going to serve you or them well. If you are able to do something, then give the interviewers this evidence. If you think you have the potential to do something, tell them that too. There is not time in the process for you to be bashful, expecting them to do the work drawing your expertise out. We have met clergy who feel a deep sense of discomfort in the interview process because they do not like 'blowing their own trumpet'. Don't think about it in these terms in the interview: if it helps, you could try seeing the process as a dispassionate interaction in which questions are being asked which you need to answer. Alternatively, don't be like this minister: 'When I told them in all due humility that I wasn't very good at anything, I didn't expect them to believe me!' Your responsibility during the interview is to allow the talents you have been given to shine.

Make sure that you do not bring with you previous experiences of interviews where you were not recommended. It does not serve you or the church to have the ghosts of past (bad) interview experiences with you in the room. This is a new opportunity to show what you have to offer this different place.

Closing the interview

Both parties need to leave the interview well and to be in the position that the other is encouraged and interested in this being a relationship that could work. If midway through the interview you suddenly feel that something is not right, it is more useful to continue trying, to continue giving evidence and requesting evidence, than to give up. Time and opportunity can be made after the interview to determine what the doubt was about, and to deal with that appropriately (maybe finding out more information). But for both candidate and selectors to make a decision while in the process of interviewing is unfair.

In closing, both parties should thank the other for the time and opportunity. The candidate may want to know when decisions are being made and when they are likely to hear from the selectors. The interviewers may be interested to know if other jobs are being applied for, and where the candidate is in that process.

Discernment and decision-making

So you have gone through the process. You have audited where your church is and what you need. You have identified how you will uncover this evidence. You need to make a decision.

Often, the interviews and auditions are back to back, one candidate after another. The danger of this is that it allows our tendency for halo and horns to reappear: one thing sticks out about the candidate and that is the thing we remember, and it is on that one thing that our decision-making hinges, particularly after a long and hard day of listening (which is something we don't often spend a whole day doing) and concentrating (another skill which we may not be used to doing for such a long period of time). With your knowledge of yourself, ask yourself honestly if when you're tired at the end of a long day is the best time to be making an important decision.

Coming to a decision

Before looking at the evidence, begin by spending time in prayer. In the quiet, prayerfully, each member notes down what they are discerning and puts the notes away until later in the process.

Step 1: Ground rules

The end of the process may seem like a strange time to be establishing ground rules, but you have not worked together like this before, and if you want to make an objective and robust decision in a focused and fair way you will need a rapid agreement on how this meeting will be effective.

Here are some suggestions: you will have others.

- *Focus*: to maintain focus all phones should be off and no interruptions should be allowed.
- *Process*: maintain the agreed process, not missing out steps to reach the decision-making phase too early. One approach to doing this – which will not be to everyone's taste – is to shout 'Keep that judgement out of the room!' when it feels as if fact is becoming judgement. You may not be comfortable shouting this to the bishop, but do make sure that there is an alternative mechanism in place by which judgement can be kept in check until the appropriate time.
- *Disagreement*: this is allowed.
- *Respect*: always respect others' opinions.

Step 2: Collating evidence

This is the point when all the evidence is gathered. It will be more effective if some basic facilitation is used to keep track. Use a flip-chart sheet for each candidate and invite panel members to add evidence against all the themes. Alternatively, use Post-it notes for each panel member to note their observations of how the candidate meets or does not meet the criteria. Most importantly, the method of gathering evidence together and decision-making needs to:

- be evidence-based;
- allow input from all members of the panel;
- be recorded in case it is challenged later.

At this stage, there is no judgement: this is only about collating evidence. Once you feel certain that all the evidence has been gathered

Table 14.3 Using all the data

	How data is used
Application form	
References	
Candidate's web presence/profile	
Hearsay	
Drive around	
Audition/presentation	
Interview	

(the chair needs to ask 'What else?' at least three times with no response to know that you've finished), move on to how you measure the evidence against your selection criteria.

Check through to make sure that you have used all the data. You may want to use a chart like Table 14.3 to ensure all data is captured.

Step 3: Who definitely does not meet our needs?

Is there anyone who does not meet the criteria from the person profile? If so, take them out of the process now. This will make the decision-making process a little lighter and easier to manage. If it is not unanimous, have a discussion about this candidate based on your evidence to decide whether to keep them in the process.

Step 4: Measuring against the person profile

Now comes the time to measure the evidence against the person profile. Of all the evidence that you have displayed on the flip-charts, which criterion from the profile does this fit? What evidence falls outside the original person profile but would be of added value to the church?

Give each criterion in the person profile an identifying letter and '+' to identify added value. Note these against your flip-chart sheets and you will quickly be able to see how the candidate meets your profile and what else they have to offer. This also allows you to check whether there are any gaps: a good candidate meets four of the selection criteria. Was there any evidence relating to the fifth? Was this missed as you collated evidence or did the candidate not demonstrate any of the required skills or experience to tick this box?

To finish the selection process, the panel needs to look at the picture they can see on the flip-charts in front of them. All the evidence that has been gathered is there and it can now be matched against the needs of the church.

Decision-making

With robust analysis, you may identify that there is one candidate who is clearly the minister you need for your church. But there may be more than one, so the decision turns into: who do we discern would be the best fit? That is about calling, competence and chemistry, and it will be important to include each person's added value.

Return to the thoughts that you had in the prayer time at the beginning of your wash-up meeting, and ask people to reflect quietly on how that fits with what is now on the wall. After a suitable time of reflection, you will be going around the room ensuring that everyone states who, based on the selection evidence and discernment, they believe has the right calling, competence and chemistry to be the next minister.

There will be discussions throughout this process. There may be disagreements. There must be discernment: everything that happens in this final stage of the process needs to be enveloped in prayer. Be aware that you may be guided by God during the night, or several hours after a conversation. You may therefore decide to make a decision and then delay communicating it to the candidates until the next day. If everyone is in agreement, allowing time and space for discernment can bring the discernment back into the centre of the selection process. This can be a challenge to diaries, but might be resolved by an early morning telephone call or emails.

At a selection event, one candidate stood out from the rest throughout the process: erudite and intelligent, she met all the criteria, and at the wash-up meeting it looked as though she was definitely going to be the successful candidate. It was decided that the panel would reconvene in the morning to confirm this decision. But by then all the members of the selection panel had changed their opinion. Although on paper she looked perfect, the panel felt they needed to have a further discussion about another candidate who also fitted the criteria. And the decision was taken to select him: it was the right decision, based on discernment and evidence from the selection criteria. The church appointed the person with the right calling, competence and chemistry for that place.

Communicating to the candidates

This part of the process may be in the hands of the regional representative, and it is not over until the candidate has also had time to discern. They may ask for 24 hours to think and then turn the job down, in which case some more thinking will need to happen.

If the answer is yes, you can start thinking with the regional representative about the next steps of announcing the appointment and looking forward to the new leader starting their work in your church. Timing is really important here and no names must be announced or implied until you have been given permission.

The process you have gone through will enable you to have fair and reasonable discussions with candidates who are not taken forward at this stage of the process. Someone – often the regional representative – will need to provide proper feedback to the candidates against the person profile so that they fully understand that they are not right for this job, right now, or alternatively can change the evidence they put forward on applications in future interviews. They also need honest feedback if their interview style did not match who they are. The Church is still learning to give honest feedback well. That's how it will become more of a learning organization.

Jesus exhorts us to love one another. There is no caveat to this which says 'unless they have applied for a job as a minister and you don't think they're suitable'. Part of our responsibility, as good Christian citizens, is to look after each other: we have seen clergy who have been damaged by poor management of the selection process.

> In the quiet . . .
> We hold up
> This decision
> To You.

Part 4

MANAGING TRANSITION AND ARRIVAL

15

Holding the community

The community changes during a vacancy. Change happens: it is a normal part of life. Expect that when a leader moves on there will be emotion. Some people will be sad and others might have a sense of relief.

Recognize this, and recognize also that it is important for the future health of a church community to manage the transition well.

How change happens: the wilderness

The Exodus story of the Israelites beautifully illustrates the natural phases of transition which accompany change and inevitably need to happen every time a leader moves on. We hope that this won't take 40 years in your church and community! The Israelites are also an early example of what happens as groups form and develop. Tuckman[1] talks about forming, storming, norming and performing. Each time a member leaves or arrives in a team, the group needs to adjust its behaviour, and this often follows the pattern known as forming (tentative beginnings with dependence on leader), storming (power struggles as people find their places), norming (clear roles and responsibilities) and performing (the team knows what it is doing and gets on with it together). With this in mind, Exodus makes interesting reading.

The first stage of transition is endings. It was time for the Israelites to move on. But they were stuck in slavery and Moses tried many times to persuade Pharaoh to let the Israelites leave Egypt. Eventually God intervened, and as the people were finally on the way to the border He was still not fully convinced that they would not turn around and stay if they faced difficulties.[2] They left through the Red Sea and told the story of their exit as they tried to make sense of where God was in what had happened.[3] William Bridges[4] talks about the importance in the change process of ending well. Until people have dealt with their losses – good or bad – they will not be ready to move on.

The second phase of transition is the neutral zone or wilderness. The walk from Mount Sinai to the Israeli border takes six days. It is probably less than a month's walk in total across the wilderness from Egypt to Israel. Yet the Israelites were wandering in the wilderness of the Sinai Desert for 40 years. It is a desolate, silent, exciting and confusing place. The Israelites were required to learn to think differently, and to hold their nerve that they would eventually reached the promised land. This in-between time resonates with some of the emotions which Elisabeth Kübler-Ross[5] talks of in the grief process after loss: anger, bargaining, depression and testing. While Kübler-Ross recognizes the risk of depression, the wilderness can also be a time of innovation and opportunity to think differently.

The final phase of transition is the new beginning. If only the new beginning or the promised land would start the day that you welcome your new minister! Unfortunately it does not and we can put huge pressure on leaders by expecting that to be true. The Israelites' new start did not begin the day they crossed the Jordan river. There were things that needed to be done together first. In your church, the real new beginning will happen a few months down the line when you are working together as community with your new minister, discovering together a new sense of purpose that makes the change begin to make sense and to work.

Measure where you are in your church story against these models (Table 15.1). Recognizing the phases of change means that you can have a better understanding of why the community or individuals may be reacting in a particular way.

Unfortunately, some churches and organizations resist the work involved in managing transition and this can lead to being unwilling to leave the past behind. Yet you cannot go back to your old leader – they have moved on. You can take some of the past with you. The Israelites took their stories and some of their possessions with them as they left Egypt. But they got stuck in the wilderness instead of moving on. What will you need to do in your church to make sure that does not happen? Kübler-Ross suggests that it is more common to get stuck in the in-between phase in what she calls 'cool' cultures – particularly in some UK cultures where it is not acceptable to express anger! When the emotions around transition are not expressed, they may be being repressed. Similarly, people can remain stuck in anger. You can sometimes see this in those

Table 15.1 Tracking your church's story

Exodus	Kübler-Ross stages of grief	William Bridges transitions	Tuckman	Our church story
Passover – Israelites were spared and told to retell the story of how God rescued them from Egypt	Shock Denial	Ending, losing, letting go		
Exodus – Israelites left Egypt in a hurry				
The wilderness	Anger Bargaining Depression Testing	The neutral zone	Forming Storming Norming Performing	
The promised land	Acceptance	The new beginning	Forming Storming Norming Performing	

who have been bereaved. You may be able to see it in your church community.

Preparing for the wilderness

Jesus spent months if not years preparing His followers to be able to manage after He had left. And when He was gone, they still weren't ready! He warned them that He would be leaving, and had made clear throughout His time with them that they had a responsibility to act and work. Yet the team's first response is to stay together.[6] That may be shock or it could be grief. It may simply be that they did not fully understand how to move forward.

The role of the church representative

The relationship between you and the church community may shift a little during the vacancy, perhaps without you noticing. As a church representative you have moved into a role where you are perceived to be the fundamental decision-maker to whom the church community has easy access. Even if you have other clergy, final responsibility during the vacancy rests with the churchwardens or deacons and the regional representatives. As well as managing activities that the minister would be responsible for, which is a major task in itself, the community in transition needs to be looked after too.

Clearly defined responsibilities can help in the wilderness time. So can planned neglect, where you decide consciously that there are things which will not happen. The Companions of Brother Lawrence, a group of missionaries working in India in the 1960s, included the following in their Rule of Life:

> For us, planned neglect will mean deliberately choosing what things we will leave undone or postpone, so that instead of being oppressed by a clutter of unfinished jobs, we think out our priorities under God, and then accept, without guilt or resentment, the fact that much we had thought we ought to do, we must leave.[7]

Endings

Good endings are as necessary for those who remain as for those who leave. Even when the general sense in a church is that a minister is well loved or well tolerated, different people will feel differently about them leaving. For your future health, it is important to manage a good ending. In most cases this will involve leaving services and parties and presentations. A good leaving means that the minister and church can be certain of what was achieved together. Both will have a legacy of each other.

Yet sometimes ministers leave unexpectedly, through illness or for other reasons, and there is no chance to manage endings properly. When this happens, you will need to consider how to manage the ending in their absence. When Polish president Lech Kaczynski was killed in a plane crash in 2010, along with a number of his colleagues, the government was left without a leader, with no preparation for managing the country and with no opportunity for goodbyes. The country went into shock and big decisions were made in a different way from normal. Without preparation for the leaving, the church community need to express their grief, concern or anger. It may be that a specialist needs to be brought in to support them, as well as ensuring there are appropriate services which mark the leaving.

In the wilderness

People can become sensitive and highly emotional in the in-between time. Irritations which could have been contained during ordinary time bubble over, and seemingly trivial details take on great importance. As a person with responsibility at this time, notice this is happening but do not add fuel to the fire by getting drawn in.

If you skim through Paul's letters to the early church you will find that nothing you will experience in your transition is new! And he has some great advice for managing the wilderness time and beyond:

- There will be bickering.[8]
- You need everyone's gifts and skills.[9]
- It is important to thank God for each other.[10]
- Know what you are here for and be united.[11]
- Be kind to each other.[12]
- Keep perspective about your own role and behaviour.[13]
- Forgive each other.[14]

It may be useful to share this in a way that is appropriate in your church context.

Exploiting the wilderness

Defining the community

Even if your community is demographically quite stable, church leaders leave. Your church may feel that the vacancy will be challenging and difficult and an interruption that could be done without. But this season is critical for your church. As well as the times when your church seems to be rolling along happily, with successful outreach activities and great worship, there must be times when you struggle.[15] This is the season of testing for your church: a particular season when your utter dependence on God is demonstrated. This is also the time when the community, without a leader, can define itself.

There is a fine dividing line between churches as followers of Christ and as followers of a particular leader. The space in between is a chance to find your identity as a community. One church lost their minister when he took on a high-profile regional role. Initially they took on his identity – basking in his reflected greatness. This dis-empowered them and they had to take time to rediscover who they were as their new minister came into post.

Telling the story

Depending on the church's previous history, during the wilderness there may be a sense of looking back with regret or with nostalgia while the present is working itself out. The Israelites too spent many hours posturing, positioning, grumbling and remembering how things used to be, including moaning about the food and the cucumbers[16] which they had enjoyed in Egypt, while in the present time they were being divinely provided for.

To manage the transition between the minister leaving and a new appointment being made, it is useful and important to acknowledge and respect the past, identify the present, acknowledge losses and explore what is coming to an end. And what is not.

One church gathered images from magazines, newspapers and postcards and invited people to pick a couple which illustrated what they thought the church was like now and what it was like when they first arrived. They used these to start a conversation in small groups and then gathered what they had learned into areas:

- What's different?
- What do we miss?
- What's good?
- What are my feelings?
- What are other people's feelings?

Through this they began to understand other people's feelings and experiences rather than just their own. They ended the encounter in a quiet and prayerful way[17] which acknowledged the gains and losses that had brought them, as a community, to this moment.

Activity

Some churches have found that focusing on particular events in the in-between time can pull people together. For example, big festivals such as Christmas and Easter are usually events involving larger numbers of people, and you probably know how to do them well. Social events and trying out new initiatives can bring the community together. Make sure these things don't stop during a vacancy! Take the opportunity to bring new people in to plan and organize: the burden needs to be shared out and this would be unmanageable alone. Newer members of the congregation or those on the fringes who baulk at a long-term responsibility in the church may be delighted to be asked to help with a one-off event. Be mindful that there will be a limit to energy and resource. One church took on a major outreach initiative during a vacancy, and there was a point at which individuals were buckling under the pressure without the safety net of the minister. However, with the grace of God it worked, and the community were stronger as a result.

Unity

It can be helpful to acknowledge the corporate responsibility which a church shares, and where it sits within the bigger context. In the Anglican communion service, there is a response which is about unity:

> This is the faith of the Church.
> **This is our faith.**

The Lord's Prayer is also a corporate prayer, which describes our needs as a community rather than as an individual. Joining together in prayer, reconciling and putting aside the differences and sensitivities which may divide is what is required of us.[18]

This process is huge for you. It is occupying a great deal of head space and prayer time. And your church is one of thousands of churches in the UK, throughout the world and through history. Churches, like clergy, are a team through time, commissioned by Jesus. That's quite a lot of corporate prayer![19]

16

The last and the first

This is where your story ends and begins. You will be writing this chapter together with your new minister over the months and years to come. You might like to photocopy these pages and fill them in.

Go in peace, to love and serve the Lord.

Notes

1 Introduction

1 Stephen R. Covey, *The 7 Habits of Highly Effective People*, London: Simon and Schuster, 2004 (first published 1989).

5 Prayer

1 Thomas Merton, *Dialogues with Silence*, San Francisco, CA: HarperSanFrancisco, 2001; London: SPCK, 2002.
2 See <http://www.creativeprayer.com>.
3 See <http://www.taize.fr>.
4 See <http://www.iona.org.uk>.

6 Where are you now?

1 Matthew 13.

7 The audit

1 See <http://www.cofe.anglican.org/about/thechurchofenglandtoday/>.
2 Chalke and Mann, 'Different Eyes', 157, 'Revelation 21' was adapted with permission by Dave Steell/Steve Chalke from 'The New Glasgow' by Doug Gay in J. Baker and D. Gay, *Alternative Worship* (London: SPCK, 2003). Quote taken from *Different Eyes Learning Guide* published by Elevation for Spring Harvest (Uckfield, Sussex: Elevation, 2010).
3 Exodus 12.24–28.
4 Numbers 11.
5 See <http://www.ship-of-fools.com/mystery/index.html>.
6 See <http://christian-research.org/what-we-do/ongoing-projects/church-check/>.
7 Robert Warren, *The Healthy Churches' Handbook: A process for revitalizing your church*, London: Church House Publishing, 2004; or see <http://www.healthychurch.co.uk/>.
8 See <http://www.ncdresources.co.uk/>.
9 For details see <http://www.bbc.co.uk/news/magazine-11427207>.
10 A Google Earth image would also work as long as it is clear enough to distinguish different roads and buildings. Mark the corners of the map on the paper so that you can reposition the image at a later date!
11 See <http://www.cofe.anglican.org/about/thechurchofenglandtoday/>.
12 See <http://www.communitymission.org.uk/resources/courses/discovery.aspx>.

13 See <http://www.faithworks.info/Standard.asp?id=2536>.
14 See <http://www.englishclub.com/vocabulary/regular-verbs-list.htm>.

11 The person profile

1 Some churches now use a form of psychometric testing to gain extra information about chemistry and style, especially around leadership and communication. We use DISC (which stands for measures of dominance, influence, steadiness and conscientiousness), and other profiles are available.

13 Preparing for the process

1 Malcolm Gladwell, *The Tipping Point*, London: Abacus, 2001.
2 Developed from ideas from Joseph Luft, *Of Human Interaction: The Johari Model*, Mountain View, CA: Mayfield, 1969.
3 Galatians 3.28.

15 Holding the community

1 Bruce W. Tuckman, 'Developmental sequence in small groups', *Psychological Bulletin*, 63 (1965): 384–99.
2 Exodus 13.17.
3 Exodus 15.
4 William Bridges, *Transitions: Making Sense of Life's Changes*, Cambridge, MA: Da Capo Press, 2004 (first published 1976).
5 Elisabeth Kübler-Ross and David Kessler, *On Grief and Grieving: Finding the Meaning of Grief Through the Five Stages of Loss*, London: Simon and Schuster, 2005.
6 Acts 1.12–13.
7 Source unknown.
8 1 Corinthians 1.11.
9 1 Corinthians 12.
10 1 Corinthians 1.4.
11 1 Corinthians 1.10–17.
12 1 Corinthians 13.
13 Philippians 2.1–4.
14 Colossians 3.13.
15 Ecclesiastes 3.1–8.
16 Numbers 11.5.
17 Useful sources of worship material: the Northumbria Community, *Common Worship Compline and Celtic Daily Prayer*, London: Collins, 2005, or see <http://www.northumbriacommunity.org/PraytheOffice/eveningprayer.html>.
18 Matthew 5.23–24.
19 Romans 12.4–5.